PRAISE FOR

Diane
TRUE SURVIVOR

"A sobering, powerful memoir of overcoming devastating childhood trauma. 'Diane' paints a disturbing story of abuse and neglect, but it's fundamentally a story of survival, hope, and reconciliation. . . . The book's writing style turns Diane's conversational interviews into a well-edited story of a powerful personal journey. This book is also a model of how to be true to oral history source material while crafting a readable story that shapes disjointed memories into a tight narrative."
—*Kirkus Reviews*

"This true story reads like a compelling novel. In sharing the details of her life, Diane gives an inspiring master class on survival, heartbreak, and forgiveness. Her resilience and determination throughout unimaginable circumstances carries through every page, leaving the reader astounded by her strength and unwavering sense of self."
—Denise Rehrig, former co-executive producer of *The Late Show with Stephen Colbert* and former senior broadcast producer of *Good Morning America*

"Compelling. Inspirational. A truly powerful story of survival. I couldn't put it down once I started reading."

—Billy Hopkins, casting director of *Sex in the City, The Butler, Precious, Fatal Attraction*

"What a story! Diane is remarkably resilient and clear-minded despite suffering some incredible life challenges. Her story is very readable and moving. It's hard to believe a person could go through so much in life and remain optimistic."

—Pierre Manigault, founder of *Garden & Gun* magazine

"It's wonderful. Brilliantly done. I couldn't stop reading. I really like the 'shape' of the book. You can feel her strength growing steadily until what amounts to a genuine victory at the end."

—Josephine Humphreys, author of *Rich in Love* and *Gal: A True Story*

"In Diane's world, the odds are stacked against her from the beginning. Yet she faces life with grit, positivity, and ultimately faith that brings love, hope, and joy. She is an inspiration to all."

—Jenny Sanford McKay, author of *Staying True*

"*Diane: True Survivor* speaks to the testament of the human spirit in overcoming adversity, abuse, and more. Yet, it doesn't stop there. It also highlights the importance of finding forgiveness in your heart and allowing one's inner grace to shine brightly."

—Stephen Panus, author of *Walk On*

"Diane is a testament to the idea that you can overcome anything life may throw at you, however unfair it may seem, and you can come out the other side without losing your basic humanity, love for life, and love of others. This is a wonderful read that I highly recommend."
—Grant Leishman, *Readers' Favorite*

"Diane's tale is gritty and raw in all the right ways. I found myself transported to her world, where the struggle for existence is very real. As a survivor myself, I believe Ward Lassoe did right by Diane's story in so many ways, not the least of which is maintaining her voice in the telling of the story."
—Nicole Kluemper PhD, author of *See Jane Fly*

"When the author met Diane, he was inspired to write her story down for others to read. His commitment to complete their shared journey is heartwarming. If you appreciate books about the strength of the human spirit in difficult circumstances, then this book is for you."
—Lyn Barrett, author of *Crazy: Reclaiming Life from the Shadow of Traumatic Memory*

Diane: True Survivor
as told to Ward V.B. Lassoe

© Copyright 2024 Ward V.B. Lassoe

979-8-88824-506-4

All rights reserved. No part of this publication may be reproduced, stored in a retrieval system, or transmitted in any form or by any means—electronic, mechanical, photocopy, recording, or any other—except for brief quotations in printed reviews, without the prior written permission of the author.

Published by

◣ köehlerbooks™

3705 Shore Drive
Virginia Beach, VA 23455
800-435-4811
www.koehlerbooks.com

Diane: True Survivor

Diane
TRUE SURVIVOR

as told to
Ward V.B. Lassoe

VIRGINIA BEACH
CAPE CHARLES

FOREWORD

I MET DIANE in 2011 in Charleston, South Carolina. We were in graduate school together, completing our master's degrees in clinical counseling. In class, I usually sat with two women, who were both named Heather. But on this day, I arrived late and ended up sitting next to Diane. I didn't realize how significant that random seat choice would be.

That day, Diane and I were teamed up for an assignment where one person was the "counselor" and the other was the "new client." For the assignment, the counselor had fifteen minutes to get a brief life history from the client. I went first and started asking Diane basic questions about her life. As she started to share information about herself, I was a bit skeptical because some of the details seemed far-fetched. As we proceeded, though, I could see that she was telling her story with sincerity and earnestness. I realized that she had overcome incredible challenges in her life. After fifteen minutes, the professor told us to switch roles. Diane was supposed to start interviewing me about my life, but that didn't happen. I kept asking her questions because the details of her life were so interesting.

After that class, I learned more about Diane in conversations during class breaks and over lunches. I joked that her life would make for a great book. Through an interesting coincidence, we realized that we both grew up in New York City during the same time period. I was living in Brooklyn, and she was in the Bronx, just ten miles away. In another coincidence, we both moved to Charleston around the same time, and again, we lived about ten miles apart. As far as we know, our paths didn't cross until we were in that class together. It would be easy to say that it was just another coincidence that we happened to sit next to each other on that specific day.

But we both came to believe that it was more than a simple coincidence. Instead, we felt that I was meant to hear her story that day.

Over the next couple of years, I saw less of Diane, but we stayed in touch. I graduated and started a private psychotherapy practice. In 2014, Diane told me about some new developments in her life. Her story had evolved from one of challenge and hardship to one of grace and forgiveness. I decided to help her write a book so she could share her inspirational story with a larger audience. She hoped it might give strength to other people going through difficult times.

We weren't sure how to proceed. This was new territory for both of us. We started meeting, and I'd ask her questions, recording our conversations. Before I became a therapist, I was a journalist, so asking questions came naturally for me. I used skills as both a counselor and a journalist in these discussions with Diane.

After we spoke, I transcribed the recordings. We had spoken for almost fifteen hours in total, so there was a lot to sift through. Sometimes, we discussed the same events in three or four separate conversations, and I was struck by the specificity and consistency (both big and small) in her stories. Her recall was remarkable, in-depth, and detailed, and she was able to paint a vivid picture of events that happened decades ago.

She was incredibly open and vulnerable, and I was surprised by her trust in the process. As a private person, this was a real leap of faith for her. She made it clear that her goal was to empower and uplift others who might be struggling. She didn't want anyone's pity.

Taking these raw transcripts and turning them into a cohesive story was a bigger task than I imagined. We joked that she had given me the pieces of a jigsaw puzzle, and it was my job to arrange them into an overall image.

I tried to organize her words to provide flow and structure, but my goal was always to stay true to her voice in all its authenticity. I kept the majority of her words but left some out. I've also changed some words for continuity, clarity, or context. It's important to note that Diane's stories and language are reflective of the time period in which these interviews were conducted, as well as her childhood and experiences, which were often heavy with emotion.

We decided to leave Diane's last name out of the story because she wanted to retain some privacy. We also changed the names of all of her friends and family.

I eventually finalized a draft, and Diane was ready to move forward with the book. I showed the draft to a few acquaintances, and they found her story compelling. We sent the draft to publishers and literary agents, but we got no interest or encouragement. We were disappointed, but we felt that we had given it our best shot. As a result, her story remained just a document on my computer for years. In 2022, a new development occurred, which reignited the spark to get the book published. If you're reading this now, I guess it finally happened.

If Diane and I hadn't been sitting next to each other in class that day, I would have never heard her life story, and this book would not have been written. I'm just glad I didn't sit with the Heathers that day.

Ward V.B. Lassoe

PROLOGUE

It was summertime in 1972, and we were living on Charlotte Street in the South Bronx. It was a really dangerous neighborhood with a lot of crime. I was young, maybe twelve or thirteen, and they were hitting me, hitting me every day. One day, my mother would hit me. The next day, it was my stepfather. Some days, they both ganged up on me. It was not an easy time. It got to the point where the beatings were just suffocating me. I couldn't take it anymore.

One night, I got a big butcher knife from the kitchen, and I decided I was going to take them out. I know it sounds crazy that a kid would try something like that, but I was desperate. I was angry, scared, exhausted, depressed. A complete mix of emotions.

We lived in a tenement building, and they had just a curtain as the door to their bedroom. I tiptoed in there with the knife and went over to my stepfather's side of the bed. They were both lying there stark naked. I had never seen naked adult people up close in my life, so I stood there staring at them for a while. I have no idea how long I stood there. I remember that their bodies were sweating because we had no air-conditioning. It was really hot that night.

I'm looking at him, and then I'm looking at my mother. They're both just spread out. I'm saying to myself, *Okay, who am I going to take out? Who am I going to hurt?* I stood there with the knife, holding it with both my hands. I decided that I was going to shove it in my stepfather's chest, but then I started thinking more about it.

I knew that if I didn't hit him in the heart, he would end up killing me. I also knew there was no way I could get them both at once. I knew as soon as I stabbed one, the other would grab me. I thought, *This is not a gun. It's just a knife.* Your mind does crazy things.

Tears were rolling down my cheeks. My eyes burned with tears because I wanted to do it. I wanted to hurt them. I wanted to hurt them the way they were hurting me. And then this voice in my head said, *Don't do it. Do not do this. You will destroy your life if you do this. And if you don't do it right, they're going to kill you. Just leave. Just leave.*

So I retreated. I ran away.

1

For the first nine years of my life, I grew up in England. It was a wonderful life with a loving family. I lived in a huge house with fourteen other children. Two were darker-skinned, and I was so naive that I thought they got burned by the sun when they were little. I really did. I remember thinking, *Wow, it must have been really hot the day they were born. Someone must have left them out in the sun for too long.*

We lived in Guildford, one of the prettiest villages in England. It was only thirty miles from London, but it felt like a world away. It was sort of a Norman Rockwell lifestyle. In the middle of town, there was the church, and right next to the church was a little, tiny cemetery. Next to the cemetery, there was the bathing pool. They called it a bathing pool in England, but it was really a swimming pool.

At the time, I didn't realize I was living in an orphanage. Nowadays, it would be called a foster home or a group home. But back then, it was called an orphanage.

All us kids were raised by Carolyn and Peter Hart, and I thought they were actually my parents. I had no clue otherwise. We all called them Mum and Pop. I was a happy, well-adjusted kid. We didn't have a lot of material things in the house. It was a simple life like those old TV shows *Little House on the Prairie* or *The Waltons*. There was always plenty of food, so we actually did better than the Waltons. We always had a lot of love in that house.

I remember every school year, we would get these new plastic rubber boots. I just loved the smell of those shiny rubber galoshes, and you couldn't have told me anything different. Those boots were made for walking. To be honest, now that I think about it, they were actually the ugliest little black things, but I loved them because we didn't get a whole lot of new things.

We had balls and stuff like that, but we didn't have all this technology crap that kids have today. We didn't have a whole lot of special dolls. I hated dolls because I was a tomboy. Us kids were very creative. We took a chicken coop and turned it into a fort, that kind of stuff. There was a hole in a tree, and I'd climb up in the tree and be the lookout person in this game we played. We'd go over to the pond and play with the tadpoles. We would also pick raspberries and eat grapes off the vines.

We lived right next door to a farm, and I had a little orange bicycle that folded in half. My parents would have me go to the farm and get the milk for the house. It came in glass bottles, and I would pedal them back home. The farm also had fields of plants and flowers that they used to give to the hospitals and church.

I also had a bunny rabbit. I loved my bunny rabbit. That probably is my earliest memory, playing with that bunny rabbit. I also remember turning over rocks and looking at the slugs. At Christmas, I remember that we had big trees in the foyer, really large ones with big glass bulbs, but they didn't blink or anything. And I remember food smells, good food smells.

The orphanage was a big, beautiful, old type of house. There were three beds to a room, so I shared a room with two other girls. Our bedroom had gigantic seven-foot windows, and the big trees outside sometimes looked like monsters at night. I would be up under the covers, scared out of my mind by the shadows from the trees. I was just a little kid.

Pop worked a lot, and he smoked a pipe. I used to get up next to him in the sitting room, and he would watch the news on television.

I didn't know what was going on in the news, and I didn't care. I just wanted to sit next to him. He would be petting me like a dog, and I was just in heaven when I was next to him. Sometimes, he'd hoist me on his lap or take me over to his desk and let me play with his stamp collection. He gave me this private, one-on-one time. He was very kind and a very loving man.

Because there were so many kids in the house, my mom, Carolyn Hart, was a multitasker. She was wonderful. She was always working, tirelessly cooking, cleaning, parenting each of us. Once in a while, she had people that came by the house and helped her out. I didn't understand who these people were at the time. She would say, "Here's cousin so-and-so." I didn't realize they weren't actual relatives. I guess there were nannies or counselors to help the Harts take care of all of us.

People would be coming and visiting us all the time. Sometimes, they would take us for a ride out into the country. We lived in the country, but they would take us deeper, deeper into the country. Then we'd have to walk back. It was just exercise, something for them to do with us on Sunday afternoon. I remember that David had bad diarrhea one time, so he had to go into the woods and wipe himself off with some leaves. Then he put his Jockey underwear on a stick and was carrying it out in front of him. We made him walk like two hundred feet behind us.

One day, I got in trouble for not coming home from school on time. I actually just went to a friend's house and forgot it was late. All of a sudden, I realized, "Wow, it's dark out there." My parents were looking for me everywhere. I had scared my mum to death. When they finally found me, she spanked me with a rolling pin. She called it spanking, but that was a joke. I think she hit me lightly twice with the rolling pin, and I cried out, "Waaaah!" Then she gave me a bowl full of strawberries and cream with sugar on it. That was the only spanking I ever got when I lived there.

The Harts had to discipline other kids in the house sometimes. David and Tony used to run around together. They would get in trouble a lot. When that happened, the two boys would get put down in the cellar for a couple of hours. I'm glad I never had to be put down in the cellar. Now that I think back on it, I guess that's not a cool thing to do to a child, to put them down in a cellar. David and Tony would get put in the cellar for a couple of hours and then be let out.

But my life at the Harts was good. I can picture myself swinging on a swing in the backyard, and I'm singing a Cliff Richard song about how happy I am. The song is called "Congratulations." It goes, "I want the world to know I'm happy as can be," blah, blah, blah. I'm just swinging up into the clouds. I'm thinking my life is great, and then it suddenly all changed.

Diane (left) with some of the other children who lived with the Harts. She's wearing her galoshes.

2

The Harts had an older daughter named Jean, who was a stewardess. She would bring home all these dolls from her travels around the world. There was a room in the house that had cabinets with all her gorgeous dolls from different countries, but we weren't allowed in that room. That was a room where my mum did all of her talking to different adults. We never knew who she was talking to.

One day, they called me to go into this room, the off-limits room. When I was told to go in there, I was surprised. I actually thought that Jean was going to show me her dolls because I had been asking her about them.

When I walked in, I saw this lady with blond hair, kind of heavyset and pretty, sitting there. My mum just proceeded to matter-of-factly tell me that this lady's name is Sharon, and she is my real mother. I'm hanging on to my mum, and I start crying when I hear this news. I'm thinking, *What are you talking about?* My mum was very weepy, and she said, "Well, Diane, Sharon brought you here when you were very little. I didn't think she was ever coming back to get you, but now she wants you back, and you have to go with her." I'm saying, "I don't want to go," but my mom said, "No, you have to go. We don't have a choice. You're going to go spend the weekend with Sharon." I was shouting, "Like hell, I'm going to go spend the weekend with her!" I didn't actually curse, but that's how upset I felt.

I'm hanging on to my mum's leg. I'm just holding on to her,

looking out from behind her at this stranger. When I walked in, Sharon was in the room sitting down, and she stood up as soon as she saw me.

Then I got another big shock when I saw that David was also in the room. He was another kid in the house who was a couple of years older than me. I had always thought of all the kids in the house as my brothers and sisters, but that day, I got a big surprise. My mom told me that David was the only one of the kids that I was actually related to. He was my real brother, and I wasn't related to any of the other kids. That was a shocker. The other kids weren't actually my brothers and sisters. It was just David and me. Him and me, we were okay, but I wasn't closest to him. I was closer to other kids in that house.

I knew that I didn't want to go away for the weekend with this woman, but I had no choice. I was really worried about my rabbit. His name was Peter, and he had red eyes. I said, "What about my rabbit? I don't want to leave my rabbit." My mum was saying, "Well, you can put the rabbit in a cage, and he will be fine."

Well, while I was away for the weekend with Sharon, the cat got to my rabbit in the barn and killed him, so I was very upset when I got home. When I found out that the cat got the rabbit, it was all too much for me to handle. I didn't see the blood or anything, but I was really, really upset. I blamed Sharon for that. If she had not come and took me away for the weekend, I would have been taking care of my rabbit, and Peter would still be alive.

The Harts had me go with Sharon for two different weekends to a flat in London. She had a friend there who had a council flat, which is like a welfare apartment, and that's where David and I stayed with her. When we got to the flat the first time, there's a little girl there. Sharon goes, "This is your sister, Mary," and I'm just looking at her. Mary was a cute little kid, only four years old. She's smiling at me, but I was too devastated to care.

I was also surprised because Mary was a different color than me. It didn't bother me because I had a brother and sister in the orphanage that were African American. Well, we didn't call them that. We actually called them colored. I just thought that if you were colored, you were born on a really hot day. I later learned that Mary's father was African American.

On the next visit back, the Harts told me that Sharon actually lived in America, not in London, and she was taking me and David back to America with her. They also told me that I had to stay with Sharon until she got all the paperwork finished. I was shouting, "No. I don't want to go to America. I want to stay with you. I don't want to go with her to America." I had no desire to come to America.

When Sharon took us back to the flat, I thought, *Okay, I'm going to run away.* But David told her that I was going to run away that night, so Sharon literally sat on top of me. She did not let me go out the door. I couldn't go anywhere. She gave me this big doll, but I didn't want it. I wanted my family. I didn't want to be with her. I didn't know her at all. I saw her two weekends, that was it, so she was still a stranger to me.

I was just devastated to realize that the people I always thought of as my parents weren't really my parents. My life was getting ready to be turned upside down. I had no clue what was going to happen. Sharon basically thought that because she was my biological mother, I would automatically love her. I did love my mother, but my mother's name was Carolyn Hart. I loved her with all my heart, and I loved my father with all my heart.

My father was shattered about what was going on. You could see it on his face. He wouldn't even come in the room, and he wouldn't go anywhere near Sharon. I was shouting, "Daddy, daddy, daddy!" He held me and told me he loved me. I was thinking, *This can't be happening. This can't be happening.* All he kept saying was "I'm sorry, I'm sorry, I'm sorry." There was nothing he could do about it. I mean, it was just like having the rug pulled out from under your feet. Everything that you thought was real was not real.

I found out later that my father died three months after I left for

America, and I really believe that he had a broken heart.

Sharon promised to take me back to see the Harts before we got on the plane to America, but she never did. I went back to see them just two times, and the third time, I was cut off, just like that. She didn't let me go back to Guildford to say goodbye to my family. Nope.

November 14, 1969. That's a date that I will never forget. I am getting on the plane to America with Sharon, David, and Mary, and I'm fighting. I'm fighting. I'm fighting. I don't want to get on the plane. I was kicking and screaming on that plane. I was literally kicking and screaming, and people were staring at me. I was very upset, full of tears. Then I got an idea. I thought, *When we get up in the sky, I'm going to ask God to help me. I'm going to tell God what's going on, and he'll do something about this.*

I had a little bit of religion because the Harts used to take us to church every Sunday. I would even dress up as an angel with wings at Christmas time. When I got on the plane that day, I was thinking, *Okay, when I get up in the sky, we will be close to heaven. When we get up there, I'm going to speak to God. I'm going to tell God I don't want this.* When we got above the clouds. I looked out the window, and I only saw clouds and more clouds. I am looking and thinking, *Where's God? Where's Jesus? Where?* I'm just a kid. This is 1969. We had only two channels on TV. There's no MTV. There's nothing to tell me how the world really is.

I was just devastated, realizing that everything was a lie. God is a lie. My family is a lie. Everything is a lie.

Carolyn Hart, David, Mary, Sharon, and Diane. She didn't realize it at the time, but this photo was taken on the last day that Diane visited with the Harts. Diane remembers being forced to hold Sharon's hand and to smile for the photo.

3

When we got off the plane from England, we were at the airport in New York City. I was still having a hard time thinking that Sharon was my mother, but then there was another surprise. There's a man waiting for us at the airport, and she introduces me. It's Sharon's husband, who was named Mack. Like I said, I'd seen a few black people before, but not as dark as Mack. He was really dark. Sharon says, "This is your new father." I said, "No, he's not." My dad was back in England.

My mom says again, "This is your dad," and I said, "No, he's not my dad." She said, "Yes, and I want you to call him Daddy." I looked at Mack, and I said, "Who's going to believe that?" Even as a little kid, I thought, *Who's going to believe that he's my dad? We're different colors. That's silly. He's not my dad.* She said, "Oh, you're going to call him Daddy," and then she slapped the heck out of me. Mack told her to leave me alone and said, "Sharon, it's okay if she doesn't want to call me Daddy right now."

I felt it was an insult to call him Dad because I already had a dad back in England who loved me, a dad that I was ripped away from. Not only was I ripped away from my family, I was ripped away from my country and from my culture. Mack was not my dad. Mack was just my stepfather, my mother's husband, and I never thought otherwise.

After he met us at the airport that day, Mack took us to Harlem.

I had no idea what I was getting myself into. This is 1969. Do you know what is going on in 1969? The civil rights movement is in full swing. Mack is black. My mom is white. That meant trouble. At the time, I didn't know anything about that because I wasn't raised around racists in England at all. I had no clue.

But now we are living with Mack's sister on 125th Street in Harlem. It's me, David, my mom, and my half-sister Mary. I learned that Mack wasn't Mary's father either. Her father was a different man that my mom had been with before she met Mack.

Mack's sister could not deal with my mother. She did not like white people. She was pro-black, and I don't blame her. White people had done a lot of bad stuff, so I can understand now what she was thinking. Of course, I didn't understand any of it back then because I was naive to everything.

In the beginning, we just stayed at the apartment all day. My mom took a while to enroll us in the local school because we had British passports. When Mack left the apartment to go to work, his sister would lock up the TV in the closet so we couldn't watch it. We would have nothing to look at all day long, nothing to do. She would even take the sugar and lock it up in a cupboard, all kinds of stupid things like that. She was just really rude. She would also argue with my mother when Mack wasn't around.

Well one day, Mack backtracked to the apartment after we thought he had left for work. When he got back, he saw the TV locked up in the closet. He and his sister got into a big argument. The next thing you know, we were out of that apartment. Mack just took whatever little money he had and moved us to Charlotte Street, which was in the South Bronx ghetto.

If you look up Charlotte Street in the South Bronx in 1969 on the internet, you will see nothing but a war-torn street. Most of the buildings were burned. They were burned down due to landlords trying to collect insurance money. The tenants knew if they got burned out of their house, they would get to move over into the projects, which was much nicer than living with the rats.

There was a huge strike by the garbage men after we moved there. The garbage was piled up on the sidewalks, and people were getting really upset. The rats were running everywhere. People took all the garbage cans and just threw them all over the street. It was horrible.

When I looked out my bedroom window at the new apartment, I could see a stairwell in the building next door. One day, I saw a man standing there. He pulled down his pants and started shaking his wanker at me. I thought he was just shaking it, but he wasn't shaking it. I realized later that he was masturbating, and I'm just looking at him. I'm nine years old, so I don't understand what's going on. I sort of go behind the curtains, but I can still see him because the curtain is sheer. He can't see me because I'm behind the curtain. I shouldn't have been seeing stuff like that as a little kid.

Whatever little money Mack had started running out, so he got a job at a computer company. My mom also ended up getting a job as a nurse's aide at a local hospital. We did eat. I can't say that I was ever starved. We didn't eat steak every day, but we were never hungry. That was never the case, but there was a lot of stress about bills. I can remember Mack and my mom arguing a lot about money. At that point, I guess I just shut down emotionally. I was depressed. I had lost my family in England, and I didn't want these people to be my parents.

England was so different than America back then. I kept wondering, *Where are the white people in the South Bronx?* I started learning a little bit about the racial tensions. When Mack would walk outside with my mom, people would say rude things to them because she was white and he was black. He would get into fights a lot. My mother did not look Spanish, so she couldn't pass for Puerto Rican. She looked Caucasian through and through. She was just not passing.

People would yell expletives at us because we're white and they're black. This was a very volatile time, but Mack was very strong, and he would fight. He would get in people's faces, and they were afraid of him. But they also did respect him. He managed to make friends with a few people in our apartment building. People liked the way he treated their children, so then they ended up just kind of accepting us.

4

In the South Bronx during this time, I stood out as a white girl with a British accent. One day, my mom tells me I'm going to third grade at PS-61. PS stands for public school. That's where I really stuck out.

After I start going there, the teachers would come into my classroom. I guess they were all talking about me. They're saying, "We've got this kid from England. You're not going to believe this." I was some kind of little spectacle or whatever. The teachers would come and talk to me because they couldn't believe that this white British kid was in the ghetto.

It was like I was on display for show-and-tell, seriously. They would say, "Well, do you know your name?" And I'd say, "Yeah, I know my name." So they'd ask, "What's your name?" And I'd tell them. They'd ask, "Do you like America?" I'd say, "No. I can't stand it. I don't like it and don't want to be here."

One day in school, they started playing this familiar tune. I recognized it right away, so I volunteered to lead the class. I started singing "God Save the Queen." I didn't realize that it's the same tune as "My Country 'Tis of Thee," and that's what all the other kids were singing. A teacher said, "Honey, we don't sing that song over here."

Another day at school, this girl told me that I should call my mother a "whore." She goes, "Oh, you need to tell your mother she's a whore. If you do that, she's going to love you. She's going to buy you candy." I have no clue what the word means. So that night, I'm sitting there eating dinner. I said, "Mom." She said, "What, Diane?" I said to her, "You're a whore."

Well, I tell you, that was not a pretty sight. She got me slammed up against the wall, just pounding me with her fist. I was tasting blood in my mouth, and my face was all puffy and swollen. When Mack came in, he also beat me because my mom told him what I said. Neither of them realized I had no clue what the hell the word meant.

The next day, I saw that girl in school, and I was so angry at her. All I could think about was revenge. I thought, *Okay, I know you're supposed to be staying in your house after school, but I also know you keep sneaking out of your house when your mama ain't home, so I'm going to get you.* I wanted payback. I was so angry. I was so full of anger at everything. I was just miserable, and I didn't care. I really didn't care.

That afternoon, I snuck into her family's apartment, carrying some newspapers with me. I knew she would leave the apartment door open when she was sneaking out of the house when her mother was at work. After I saw her go outside, I went upstairs, put some newspapers under her bed, and lit them with a match. I watched until the paint on the windows started melting, then ran back outside.

She was out there, and I said, "Hey. Look at your bedroom. There's smoke," and she yelled, "Oh, my God!" She ran to the fire alarm. The fire trucks came. Her mother beat the hell out of her because the fire people said it started because she was smoking in her bedroom. That's what I wanted. I wanted her to hurt the way I was hurting when they beat the living shit out of me. Her family ended up moving to the projects.

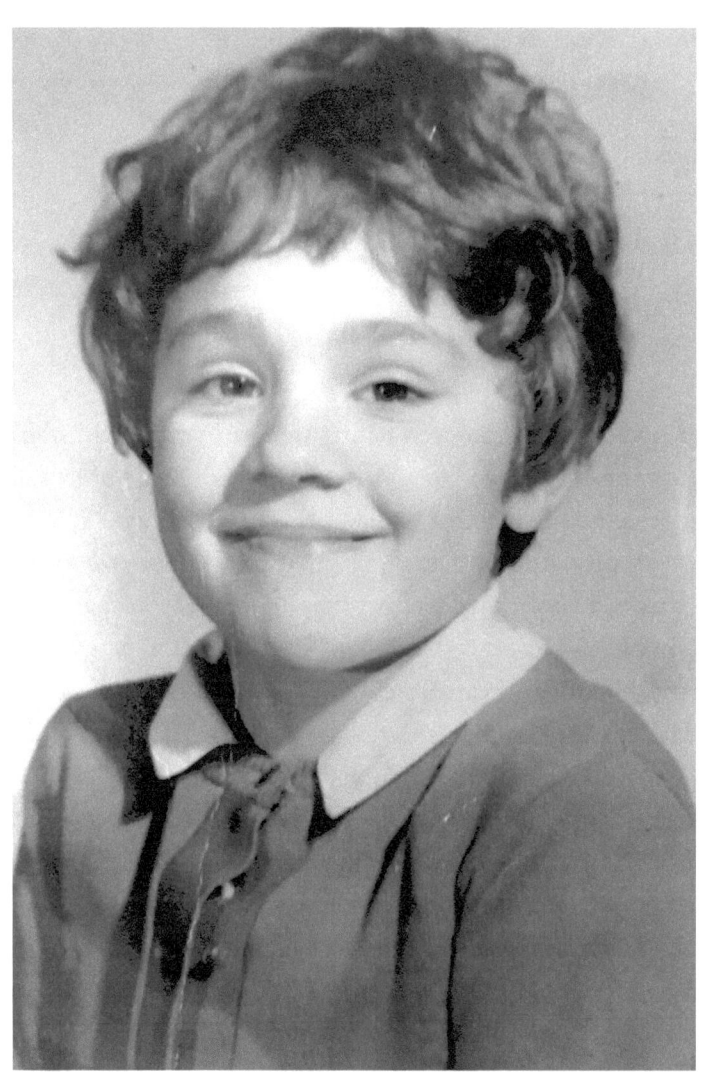

Diane's third-grade photo, her first year in America

5

My brother had an even harder time than I did with the move from England to New York. David was a boy, but he sounded like a girl. And the fact that we had British accents made it worse. He would get picked on in school all the time. He was two years older than me, but I was out there fist-fighting for my brother. I was the tomboy, but David would be crying, "Oh, Mommy!" when other kids were mean to him. "I can't take it anymore. I've got to go. I've got to go." He didn't realize that you can't go out there in public talking like that, so I would go out there and fight for him.

Then it got really bad at home. It started to happen between David and Mack. He thought he could make my brother into a man, so he started physically abusing David. He was hitting him, punching him, and my brother would cry. Mack would get enraged. I'm thinking, *Well, you punched him. You punched a kid, and he's only twelve years old. You are 250 pounds. What do you expect him to do?*

My mother would also hit us and antagonize Mack until he hit us. Her famous words were "Wait 'til your father gets home." When she said that, my brother would heave his guts up. My brother was gay. He was a young boy with a British accent and female tendencies, gestures, and everything, so Mack was abusive to him. I was the tomboy, and I used to take the rap for my brother because I couldn't stand the way Mack beat him. I mean, Mack beat me, but he would never beat me to the point where he would beat my brother. One time, David stole a rubber ball from the store, and Mack found out about it. When he got caught, David told Mack that I stole it. This felt like such betrayal, but he was afraid, so I took the beating.

I think that he also beat my brother because he was prejudiced against gay people. He called my brother a "faggot." Mack would yell at my mother, "Your son, the faggot." My mother would say, "Don't call him that," and he was yelling, "Your son's a faggot." He had no respect for my brother whatsoever.

When I heard this argument, I was thinking, *What's a faggot?* I didn't even know that word. My mother told me, "Mack calls David that because he sounds like a girl." I told her, "Well, no, that's how everyone sounds over in England." I tried to explain it. But they were saying, "You better tell him not to talk like that," and I knew that meant they were about to kick his ass. And I'm thinking, *Nobody's gonna hit my brother. You're not gonna hurt him.* I was very much his protector.

Mack would say to David, "You're such a sissy." He would beat on David relentlessly. I could see my brother breaking down emotionally. He would be hiding in the bathroom, and my mother would say, "Oh, wait until your father gets home." David would be in the bathroom heaving, throwing up. And I was thinking, *Oh, my God!*

One day, Mack hit David while we were sitting outside of our building. David looked kind of Puerto Rican because he had an olive complexion. All the Hispanic men came running over when they saw Mack hit David. They surrounded Mack, and they were going to beat the living shit out of him because they thought he was hitting a Puerto Rican kid. So Mack sends me, stupid me, to go get my mother. I got her, and she told these guys, "No, no, that's my husband, and he's my son." They told her if they ever saw Mack hit David like that again, he'd be sorry. That's what they told them. After that, he only hit David indoors.

One time, when Mack was punching my brother, he hit the wall and broke it. The wall was made of plaster. It wasn't a sheetrock wall, and he broke his hand. I was thinking, *Oh, my God. This man's going to kill my brother!*

Eventually, my brother ran away because he couldn't take it anymore. It was another day of "Wait 'til your father gets home," and my brother just couldn't take it. He went downstairs to take out the trash and never came back. I didn't see him again for a couple of years.

6

At home, it was always "Wait 'til your mother gets home," or "Wait 'til your father gets home." Now that David wasn't living with us anymore, all their attention was on me. I guess they never hit Mary because she was so much younger. It was just me. My mom would beat me, and then he would beat me. I was stressed out the whole time. I'm in the bathroom, throwing up, having diarrhea, sweating. I mean, it's just ridiculous. They wanted to beat me all the time. They would hit me with an extension cord, a braided extension cord. *What is wrong with these people?* He'd be holding me down so I couldn't breathe.

One day, I must've said something my mother didn't like, and she went ballistic. She hit me with a cast-iron frying pan. She didn't have to hit me hard to do a lot of damage. I ended up with a cracked tooth in my mouth. After that, every time she hit me in the mouth, she would bust my lip. That was pretty crazy.

I had nightmares because of that tooth. They couldn't afford to fix it, so I kept getting temporary repairs. The fake tooth would stay in for a couple of weeks, but eventually, it would *ping* and pop out. Then I'd look like a witch because I was missing a front tooth. That was hard because all the other kids would make fun of the missing tooth.

Mack would say, "Who the fuck do you think you are? You're a nobody. You're nothing." If I dared say I was somebody, he'd smack the shit out of me. Eventually, I started believing I was nobody because that's what he kept telling me. The beatings made it hard to learn in school. I felt I was incapable. One day, he quizzed me on my multiplication tables. I couldn't tell him what nine times nine was, and he punched me in my face. I tasted blood all the time. *How do you expect somebody to learn math if you got them tasting blood every time they give you an answer?* I was fearful to try to learn math.

One day, he had me on the floor beating me. He had his knee in my back and was suffocating me at the same time. How in the world can you beat somebody and suffocate them at the same time? I'm trying to catch my breath, and then something weird happened. I didn't feel anything anymore. It was almost an out-of-body experience. I could feel it, but I couldn't feel it. Something told me to relax, even though I couldn't breathe. It was like instinct. As soon as I moved my head, I could gasp for air. How the hell can you live like that? He would beat me within an inch of my life. What is the name when you intentionally try to murder somebody? What do you call that? First-degree murder? That's what it felt like.

I can't watch football to this day because every time there was a break in the football game on TV, Mack would beat me with this wooden walking cane. One time, there was a commercial he didn't like, and he beat me worse than usual with that cane. That was the only time I ever heard my mother tell him he went too far. That's the only time I heard those words: "You went too far this time." That was the absolute worst day of my life. It was so hard because I knew there was an ocean between me and my real family. But I couldn't go back there, even though I wanted to run away, run back to the Harts. That's a seven-hour trip over the ocean by plane, you know. I knew I was stuck like Chuck.

I honestly believe my mother was actually excited to watch him hit me. That was one of the most profound, painful parts. Here I was, maybe ten years old, and they've got me down on the bed. I'm maybe 70 pounds, and Mack's 250. My mother's a big woman. She's trying to pull my underwear off to let him hit me on my bare ass. Why do you need to pull off my panties? Why do you need to do that? She's trying to pull down the only part of decency that I had left.

She made me their servant. I washed his clothes, ironed her uniforms, did everything. I was their housemaid. She made me do everything for them. I had to make their bed and pull his underwear and her panties out of the bed. They didn't even respect me enough to take their underwear out of the bed. I had to look at my mom's cruddy underwear and his cruddy underwear. They beat me so much. Let me tell you, there were days that I prayed to die. I'm not going to lie. I prayed to die. I said, "God, take me now. Take me. You can really take me because I can't take this anymore."

She also made me care for Mary like she was my kid. That's how they treated me, like I was Mary's nanny. She and I would play double Dutch. She'd be in her white socks, and my mother would literally make me scrub her socks afterward because I let Mary take her sneakers off. *Really? I let her?* I didn't let her do anything. And my mother would put bleach in the water, and I'd end up with bloody fingers, you know, from scrubbing. I knew if I didn't scrub those socks clean, she was gonna hit me.

One time, she told me to clean the house, and I was looking at the house and thinking, *There's nothing wrong with the house, so there's hardly anything to clean up.* When she came back, she got angry and hit me. She yelled, "You didn't clean the house, blah, blah, blah." Then she said, "I'm going back out, and you better have this house clean." By then, I was pretty pissed off, so I didn't do a thing. I didn't clean anything. When my mom came back, she smiled and said, "Why didn't you do it like this the first time? This is exactly what I wanted." I said to myself, "She is certifiably crazy." Right then and there, I knew she was crazy. I understand why kids kill their parents.

I used to get hit for stupid things every day. I didn't have to do anything. I'm serious when I say I got hit every day. Every single day. Yellow bruise on top of blue bruise, extension cord marks. It was every freaking day. The only day I didn't get hit was Christmas Day. It's the only day she was nice. It was crazy because they would buy us a bunch of stuff. Then after Christmas, she'd give Mary all my stuff. She'd say, "Oh, you don't need this doll. You won't play with it." I'd say, "But it's mine. It's not fair that you're just going to give my sister all my stuff."

My mother loved Christmas and would go all out on Christmas. She did. That was the only day I didn't have to clean. I used to be so tired of cleaning. I used to love to see my bed at night. I felt like a slave. I literally felt like a slave. By the time I hit the sheets, I slept so good because she worked me like a dog.

I remember that I sucked my thumb forever. That was my only vice. Really. It was my only comfort. My mother never comforted me. She never told me she loved me.

It just got to the point where the beatings were suffocating me. I'm claustrophobic to this day. I used to think that when I die, I don't want to be buried because I'd be stuck in a box. I'm thinking, *What if I can't get out?* I'm growing out of that fear. My love for the Lord has taught me that this is just flesh, and when I die, my spirit is going to Heaven, so it doesn't matter if I'm in a box. But at that time, I was terrified.

7

One day, I thought, What can I do to make them not beat me today? I knew they loved their material possessions, so I decided to set the apartment upstairs on fire as a distraction.

There used to be a lady who lived above us. I would babysit for her sometimes. She was always running around in the streets. She was seeing this one guy, and she thought she was going to keep him around by having his baby, but it didn't work. He left her, and she ended up not taking care of the baby. The baby died, so that was messed up. Then she moved out, and it was an empty apartment upstairs.

I went up there one day and took two bags of newspapers. I was maybe twelve years old. There were a couple of things in the apartment, including an old couch, and I set it on fire. Then I just left. The next thing I knew, there was a lot of screaming and yelling, and the firemen arrived.

Downstairs, my mother's running everywhere, pushing chairs here and there, doing all this crazy stuff. And the water's just coming down from the apartment up above, and the firemen are telling her, "Get out, get out!"

This neighborhood lady comes over and tells the firemen that she saw me going into the apartment upstairs and that I must have set the fire. Well, it turns out that Mack actually stood up for me that day. I couldn't believe it, but he really took up for me. He said, "She wouldn't do that. She didn't do that."

Yes. Yes, I did.

8

Over the years, I learned more about my mother's history. I found out that she was born in England. She told me she had been abandoned by her biological parents, so she also grew up in an orphanage. She wanted to be adopted, but that never happened.

She never had anything of her own that was new. She grew up during World War II, so there was a lot of rationing and shortages in England. Sometimes, the American soldiers would give her cocoa and stuff like that. She really liked the soldiers, but the nuns in the orphanage were very brutal to her. There was no compassion from those nuns. They would hit the kids in a heartbeat.

At night, all the kids would be sleeping in those rows of beds in the orphanage, and my mother would be telling the other girls, "I'm going to America when I grow up." They'd yell, "Shut up, Sharon. You ain't going nowhere." But she proved them wrong. She ended up getting to America.

The orphanage put her out in the world when she was fifteen. She went to work in a rug factory, and the men there took advantage of her. When they realized she had no family, she was put into prostitution. She was just put out there into the world, and unfortunately, the scum of the earth, the pimps, got ahold of her and almost destroyed her.

She witnessed somebody get shot in the head right in front of her. She was nineteen when it happened, and she was scared to death. She was scared the killers were going to find her and shoot her. They killed this guy in front of her, just shot him right in the head. She told me these stories, and I know they're true because of the way she tells them. It's always the same story, and it never changes. I know she's telling me the truth.

At one point, my mother was a high-class escort. My mother was hot. She was five-eight, a Marilyn Monroe type, with blond hair. She had a *wow* factor. I'm an ugly duckling compared to her. But it was all prostitution. I don't know if you've ever heard of the Harlem Globetrotters, but one of them used to take my mother out every time he was in London. This guy had a woman in every port, but he treated my mother very well. He paid her well. He bought her bracelets with charms and all kinds of stuff.

My mother ended up in London working in a brothel run by guys who were part of the Maltese Mafia. They came to London from Malta, a small country off the coast of Italy. They ended up controlling a lot of the local sex businesses in London. They were violent mobsters and pimps, and they ran large prostitution rings. My mother ended up getting pregnant by one of the pimps when she was twenty, and she had my brother, David. Two years later, she got pregnant by another pimp and had me. She knew who our fathers were because all her customers had to use a condom when they had sex with her. The pimps didn't bother using condoms when then forced her to have sex with them.

After she gave birth to me, she kept working as a prostitute. She would take us kids to the babysitter each day, like she was going to a downtown job. But instead, she was going to an apartment to meet with her johns, sometimes having sex nine, ten times a day. That couldn't have been fun, you know? And I'm sure it messed with her psyche.

I never met my biological father. All I know is that he was Maltese. People from Malta have kind of an olive complexion, so that's why I can pass for Puerto Rican. He was a pimp. He was not a good person from what my mother tells me, but I'm still just curious. I would like to talk to him one time, but that will probably never happen.

My biological father was abusive to my mom. She couldn't take it anymore, and she decided to kill herself. It was a few months after I was born. She went home to her flat one night, turned on the gas stove, but didn't light the burner. She just let the gas fill up the apartment. She put me and David in front of the stove alongside her. She tried to kill me, herself, and my brother. If it wasn't for the landlord painting the walls in the hallway, we wouldn't be having this conversation. He smelled the gas coming from the flat and kicked the door in. He saved all of us.

After that, my mom was sent to a mental hospital for several years. They called them asylums back then. She could have been arrested and charged with trying to kill her kids, but they sent her to the asylum instead. She told me that she tried to kill us because she didn't want us to suffer through the system like she did. She was worried about what would happen to us if she killed herself and left us alone. She was raised by those mean, horrible nuns. She didn't want that for us and didn't want the life of prostitution for me.

When she was sent to the mental hospital, David and I got put in the orphanage with the Harts. I was with them since I was just a few months old, so that's all I knew.

After my mom left the asylum, she met an American soldier stationed in England. His name was Bill, and he was African American. He was very abusive to my mom because he knew she didn't have anybody else to rely on. After she met him, they moved together to the United States, and she got pregnant. One day, Bill threw her down the stairs when she was almost nine months pregnant. She lost the baby. Even though the baby died, they named him Sean. I still think of him as my brother.

Afterward, the doctor said, "Well, the best thing you can do is try to get pregnant again," so that's what they did, and that's when she had my half-sister Mary. They stayed in America for a while but then moved back to England. Bill was a drug addict, and he was beating my mother a lot. Eventually, she called the police and told them where

Bill's drugs were hidden and that he was beating her. The police took his drugs and put him on a plane to America. They got rid of him because he was not an English citizen and had a record of selling drugs. That's how she got Bill out of her hair.

Then my mother met my stepfather, Mack. He was also an American soldier. They met at a place called the Douglas House in London. It was a hangout spot that all the American military guys used to go to. It was somewhere for them to relax off the base. Mack was enamored with my mom almost from the time he first met her. He wined and dined her. Then he got her a really nice apartment where she could live with Mary.

I had a revelation as she told me these stories about her past. During this whole time that she was back in England, she never tried to visit me and David once, even though we were living less than an hour away. She made no effort. How crazy is that?

Later, she moved to New York City with Mack. When she left England, she had a record for prostitution. By coming to America, she didn't have a police record to deal with anymore, so she could start over.

One Christmas at the Harts, I got a doll in the mail, and David got this gigantic, three-foot Johnny Seven gun with plastic bullets. I thought his present was the coolest thing. At the time, I didn't realize the stuff was coming from America from my mother. The Harts didn't tell me that, and they were probably wrong for not telling me. They should have told me. The Harts probably didn't think my mom was ever going to come back to England. I think that's why they didn't tell us.

One day, the Harts reached out to my mom. They told her they wanted to legally adopt me. I didn't realize this at the time. When my mom found out about their plans, she told them, "You cannot have Diane." The Harts told her, "But we've had Diane since she was a baby." But my mom said, "Absolutely not. You can't have her." I guess this conversation prompted her to come back to England to get me.

If all of that happened nowadays, my mom would have lost all her rights to claim me. It's called TPR, termination of parental rights. I would have been out of my mother's life, and so would my brother. You know that. They would have never allowed her to move to America, have another family, linger all those years, and then come back nine years later and say she wants to be Mommy. I resented that. I definitely did resent it.

9

The next school I went to in the Bronx was called Tremont Avenue Elementary. It was a modern education plan with an open floor. It was a nice building, and they had some experimental programs. My science teacher, Mr. Kantrow, was Jewish, a white guy, and very sweet. One day, I came into class with the imprint of Mack's hand on my face because he had hit me hard the night before. Mr. Kantrow realized I was being beaten, and he actually went to the principal to report it. At first, I tried to protect my mother and Mack. I told the principal I fell. I gave them all kinds of excuses.

But when she saw my face, the principal, Miss Warren, wouldn't let me go home. She called my house, and my mother said, "You better send my daughter home, blah-blah—" Miss Warren said, "Your daughter has been physically abused, and I'm going to keep her here at school until Social Services can come to get her. If you want to call the police, you go right ahead and call." Of course, my mother didn't call.

The Bureau of Child Welfare ended up giving me back to my mother after a couple of days, so it made no real difference. But it felt good to know that someone cared enough to try to help me. It seemed like Miss Warren was the first person who had really cared about me since I came to America. As I look back on my life, I've had a series of people who stepped in and helped me out when I was struggling. I call them my angels. I feel like Miss Warren was the first of the angels.

Dede was another angel. She was Mary's grandmother, and one

summer, she came to visit us. The relationships get kind of confusing here, but Dede was the mother of Mary's father. Remember, his name was Bill. Since Mary and I had different fathers, I wasn't actually related to Dede. She was only Mary's grandmother, but she always acted like a grandmother to me. When Dede came to visit, it was summertime, and I was wearing this long-sleeved sweater. When she saw me with the sweater on, she said, "Diane, sweetie, why do you have that long sweater on?" She pulled my sleeves up. She saw the bruises, and I could see the tears well up in her eyes. Then she pulled my sweater down and patted my hand. She went back to Pennsylvania, and the next thing I know, Child Welfare is back at our house. Even though I wasn't related to her, Dede cared enough about me to try to get some help. She must have known it might piss off my mom and Mack, but she did it anyway. She was another angel who helped me out at different times in my life.

The folks from Child Welfare took me for a couple of days again and then just brought me back home. I have no idea what was going on during that time while I was in a temporary foster home. All I know is that I kept ending up back with my mother and Mack. That's what they would do—take me for a couple of days and then put me right back with them. It wasn't like it is now, not at all. I know the system isn't great now, but I don't think kids would end up back in the home so quickly when they're clearly being abused. Back then, I felt like they were just going through the motions.

There was so much abuse that I just didn't want to live. I was so depressed. I mean, day in and day out, they hit me.

I remember my mom sending me to the laundromat to clean all the clothes. We had a shopping cart for the dirty laundry. She would pile up the laundry so high that it was even taller than me, and I had to drag the cart up the hill to the laundromat. One day, the wheel broke, so now I'm really dragging the cart. It was horrible. I mean, you can laugh at that stuff now, but it was not right.

She never gave me enough money to wash and dry the clothes.

But if I brought them back wet or damp, she would beat the crap out of me. So I would try to catch other people's dryers as they took their stuff out to use the rest of their drying time. But that process took a while. I would end up being gone longer than my mom expected, so she would beat the hell out of me for that.

One day, my mother couldn't find two towels after I got back from the laundry. Well, guess what? She never put them in the laundry in the first place. That's why she couldn't find them. But she beat the hell out of me because she thought I lost two of her towels. I mean, it was just ridiculous. Then, later, she says, "Oh look, I found the towels." As I'm wiping the blood off my lip, I'm thinking, *I'm glad you found the towels.*

10

I had thought about running away many times, but I always stayed for Mary, who was six years younger than me. I loved her. I could have been jealous of her because they never abused her. I'm not sure why that was. Maybe it was because she looked more like she could be their actual child. She was a mixed-race child because Bill was African American. Mary looked like she could be Mack's kid. For a while, Mary thought Mack was her father, and I didn't let her think otherwise because I didn't want him to hurt her.

The first time I decided to actually try running away, I was probably thirteen. Mack beat me once that day, and then my mom told me he was going to beat me again when he came home, so I just ran away. When David left, he said he was going to take out the trash, and he never came back. That night, I heard a voice in my head saying, "It's time for you to take out the trash." I don't know where the voice came from, but it was more than a random thought. At the time, I didn't have any sense of religion or faith. But now, as I look back, I feel like there was a Higher Power involved. I believe it was God speaking to me. It gives me comfort that He was with me even during the tough times.

After I heard the voice that night, I went to the stairwell with the trash, and somehow, Mary knew I was leaving for good. I don't know how, but somehow, she figured it out. She begged, "Diane, please don't go. Diane, Diane." But I'm running down the stairs, and she's yelling, "Diane, Diane." And I'm crying and running because I can't stay there. I can't do it anymore. I just can't stay there anymore.

I didn't know where I was running. I got to the highway near our apartment. The highway is down in a valley, and then there are all these boulders and rocks on the side. Here I am, climbing down the boulders. I could have killed myself. Where the hell was I going? I had no clue. Cars blew their horns at me. I didn't know where I was going.

Then I got scared because it got dark, and I decided I had to go home. I couldn't survive out there. But I was worried about what would happen when I got home. I'm thinking, *What can I do to make Mack not hit me?* So I decided to take a bottle and cut my leg. Back then, we had glass bottles instead of plastic. I broke the glass, and I cut my leg up the side in the thigh area. I still have the scar.

My leg was bleeding, and I took some dirt and rubbed it on my face. I actually took it to the point where the granules in the dirt were cutting me. Then a police car rolled up next to me, so I made up this incredible story that I was kidnapped by this man with an orange shirt. I told them he grabbed me, threw me in his car, and drove me around. I had so many bruises because of Mack that the police didn't figure out I was lying. They thought somebody really did attack me.

When I got home and told my story, Mack wanted to kill somebody. That was the crazy part. That man would never let anybody hurt me, but he had no problem hurting me himself. That was the insane part. He really did believe that somebody did this to me.

There was nothing but black and Puerto Rican people in the Bronx, so I had to say if it was a Puerto Rican or black guy who threw me in the car. Mack knew I would never get in a car with a Puerto Rican guy, so I had to say he was black. I told him that the guy threw me in a car and made me lie on the floor in the back. I told him that when we were stopped at a light, somehow I got out of the car. I don't know how. I just started running. Thankfully, he believed my story. I didn't get beaten that night.

Since running away didn't work that time, I knew I had to have a better plan next time. I was thinking, *I got to find someplace to go.* So the next time I ran away, I stole 300 dollars, and I thought that would last a long time.

I went to the stairwell, and Mary could tell I wasn't coming back again. She cried, and she said, "Don't leave me. Please don't leave me." And I said, "I'm sorry. I'm sorry." I was crying, and she was crying. "Please, please, don't leave me." I said, "Mary, I'm so sorry. I can't do this anymore."

This time, I stayed in the streets for two weeks, at different places. I couldn't stay with friends because my mom knew all the people I knew, so I would go into hospitals and sit next to people in the waiting room. I'd make it look like I was part of their family. I'd see people grieving and sit next to them. The hospital workers didn't have a clue. I'd go to the bathroom and shower, not shower exactly but wash up. Or sleep in the bathroom and put my body against the door and lock it. People would try to get in the bathroom and think it was locked. I also used to sleep on the subway, riding it back and forth.

One day, I was in a park, eating a bucket of Kentucky Fried Chicken. I made friends with a dog. It became my buddy. But then it got on my nerves after the chicken was gone.

I knew my science teacher, Mr. Kantrow, lived in Brooklyn, and I wanted to see him. I don't know what I was thinking. I wanted to live with him. I don't know why. I guess because he was one of the few people who was nice to me. He affirmed me. He told me I wasn't stupid. He told me, "You can learn this. You're not dumb." I figured out where he lived by looking up his name in the phone book. I went to his house. Boy, was he surprised when he saw me at his front door. He said, "Diane, you can't do this. You can't stay with us." So I ran away before he could call anyone. I went back to the park, thinking, *What am I going to do now?*

I was sitting on this stone fence, and a Jamaican-type person—he sounded West Indian—came up to me and asked me if I wanted some Chinese food. At this point, I'm hungry and tired. I've had my panties on for two weeks with no real bath. I didn't realize this guy had been eyeballing me for a while, actually watching my comings and goings.

At that point, it was just ridiculous. My sneakers smelled so bad. I had Pro-Keds on. I had only washed up in hospital bathrooms. I was tired. I guess my spirit was giving up. This guy said, "Well, you can come and stay with me. You could spend the night." He told me he had a room I could stay in, so I'm thinking this man has a real house.

No, it turns out this man has only got one room, with a bathroom and a kitchenette—like a studio apartment. When we get to his place, there was no room for me. The bed was up against the wall. And I'm thinking, *Oh, my God*. I'm eating Chinese food, and my survival mode kicks in. I remember that Isaac Hayes song "Chocolate Chip" playing on the radio. The next thing I know, he's walking around with only his red Fruit of the Loom underwear on. And God, I couldn't help but look at his junk. I was thirteen, still a virgin, and his junk looked huge. I was scared of it.

He's walking around with his underwear on. He gave me one of his T-shirts, so now I'm in his T-shirt and my raggedy panties. The T-shirt's long enough to cover me though. He put my sneakers outside the window on the ledge—that's how badly they smelled. He let me take a shower and everything.

Then I'm in the bed, pressed up against the wall, as he's walking around the room. Then he gets into the bed next to me. So here he is, and I'm next to him. I tried to push myself through that wall, but there was nowhere for me to go. I'm just thinking, *What can I say to him to make him not want to hurt me?* I realize that he got me here to his apartment, and I got nowhere to go. He told me he had a house and a safe place for me to sleep, but now I realize it's me and him sharing the same bed.

So I started talking. I tell my story and cry. I told him what Mack did to me and how my mom abused me. I'm showing him the marks on my arms and stuff. I told him, "God is going to bless you for helping me." Well, let me tell you, when I finished, that man said,

"Let me just go to sleep," and he didn't do anything to me. He woke me up the next morning and told me I had to leave. When I got outside on the street, I said, "Thank you, God. I'll never do that again. I promise I'll never do that again."

I went home, and they weren't as angry as I expected them to be. But I kept running away. One day, I climbed up in a tree in a park and slept there. Seriously. A police officer saw me and said, "Sweetheart, you could get hurt sleeping here in this park. You need to go home." I said, "Look, I'm safer in this park than I am at home." He was dumbfounded and said, "Okay, don't go anywhere. Let me see what I can do."

He tried to get me into an emergency group home, but I told him I'm not going to any group home. I said, "You can take me there, and as soon as you leave, I'm out the door. I'm not staying there." I wouldn't tell him who I was or where I lived. He was saying, "You have to tell us who you are," and I said, "No, because you'll take me back home. I'm not telling you anything. I'd rather be locked up." He said, "You know they can lock you up for running away," and I said, "That's fine. I'll be safer locked up." And I was safer.

11

David had been gone a couple of years, but I managed to track him down through mutual friends. I found out he ended up in prostitution. He had been dancing and stripping at gay bars to survive. Eventually, a bunch of drag queens found him living on the streets, and they took care of him and mothered him. I think David fell in love with those drag queens. Their names were Peaches and Wendy. They dressed him up in nice clothes, and they took care of him. They lived in high-end apartments, but my brother was paying a heavy price because he was having sex with them

They were prostitutes, but they were very well dressed. They weren't the kind of transvestites who went around on 'Ho' Avenue. That's a nickname for a street in New York with a lot of hookers. They were more like downtown prostitutes. They were the type to hang out with the closeted gay people, that kind of stuff. They had Calvin Klein and Sasson jeans and all the name-brand stuff. As David grew into manhood, he started protecting them. He stood there while they turned tricks, and he made sure nobody hurt them.

After we reconnected, David would let me know where he was sometimes, and I would go see him. Even though he was running around with drag queens, he had a room in their apartment that looked like it belonged to a little kid. It had teddy bears and stuff like that. I was thinking, *Oh, Lord!* I was probably about thirteen, and I knew something wasn't right for a sixteen-year-old boy to be living like that.

He would get defensive when I tried talking to him about being a prostitute for adult men. David said, "Diane, they're not having sex with me. I am just doing it to them." I said, "David, that's still gay, whether you're doing it or he's doing it." My brother claimed that he wasn't gay. He said he had sex with them, but they never penetrated him. I tried to explain that if you're doing that kind of stuff, you're gay. That's kind of how our conversations went.

One of the drag queens, Peaches, was jealous of me because she didn't believe that I was actually David's sister. My brother and I don't look that much alike because we had different fathers. My brother looks much more Italian. David kept telling Peaches, "Diane's my sister," but she didn't believe him.

At one point, I was put in a group home, and David was in another group home. I guess Social Services got him off the streets for a bit. He called me and told me they were doing an operation on him, and they were going to circumcise him. I started crying and telling other people in the group home, "Oh, my God, my brother needs to have surgery." I'm young and stupid, and the people in my group home are asking, "Well, what are they going to do to him, Diane?" I said, "They're going to circumcise him," and they just burst out laughing. I had no clue what they were doing to him, so they explained it to me.

The social workers allowed David and me to see each other. He told me he wasn't going to stay in a group home. He said, "I'm not staying here. I'm just going to leave again." And that's what he did. He went back on the streets. We knew people in common, so, over the years, I would hear about him sometimes. So-and-so would say, "Oh, I saw your brother, and he lives here now," or "He's living there." Sometimes, people would tell David, "I saw your sister, and she's living here." We would kind of find each other that way. Even though we were living different lives, he was the only person who really understood our childhood back in England. That was comforting.

He kept working as a prostitute to support himself, but he seemed to be holding it all together. Until he got into drugs.

12

I had thick, beautiful hair when I was young. I was one of those thirteen-year-old girls that looked nineteen. It must have been something in the milk, I don't know. I didn't do anything to make myself that way. I might have put a little Dippity Do in my hair, just a little gel. It turned my hair into kind of a wet Afro.

At that point, I started to become who my mother used to be in terms of looks. As I became more attractive, she resented it. She was very overweight at that point. My mother probably ballooned to about 260 pounds, and I was this little, tiny, twenty-four-inch waist thing with boobs. But I didn't wear tight-fitting stuff or flaunt my looks. I didn't wear short skirts or anything. I just liked my jeans.

But I could tell my mother was getting jealous of me and worried about her marriage to Mack. She'd beat the hell out of me, saying, "Are you trying to look sexy for him?" I'd just be sitting there reading a book. She'd say, "Oh, you think you're all so-and-so." I mean, I couldn't do anything right. She just looked at me like I was her adversary.

She got more and more angry at me. She'd come up behind me and snatch me by my hair. "Oh, you think you're being cute for him," and she'd beat the hell out of me before Mack got home. It was just hell.

Well, eventually, her fears became my reality.

Around that time, I noticed that Mack started trying to be my buddy. He was saying, "You know what, Diane? I won't let your mother hit you." He promised me he would never let her hit me again, but he made it clear that I had to do what he wanted me to do.

One night, he came into my room and told me he wanted to talk to me. It was a night when my mother was at work. He pulled out a shoebox, and he had a big bag of weed in it. It wasn't a full ounce, but it wasn't just a ten-dollar bag either. He started rolling up a joint and offered me some. Right away, my defenses went up, and I was on guard. I knew he was up to something. I was thinking, *He's going to try to get with me. He wants to bring down my inhibitions and my walls of resistance. He wants to take advantage of me.* I figured it out real quick.

I had no choice but to smoke it, but I did a Bill Clinton. I purposely did not inhale. I was very afraid of what he was going to do to me, and I was also trying to make as much noise as I could to try to wake up my little sister, who was sleeping on the other side of the room. He tried to tongue kiss me, and I bit down on my lips. His tongue was all over my mouth. Eventually, he said "okay" and backed off. But then he said, "I'll show you one day."

He kept at it. I would be in the kitchen unpacking the groceries, and he would run his hand up my leg. Or he would come into my room again at night. Usually, I'd be able to wake up my sister. He would say to Mary, "Go back to bed," but eventually, he would get pissed off and leave me alone.

A few weeks later, he really made his move.

It all started when a girl in my class skipped school one day. Her name was Diane Forman. The school called my mom and said, "Do you have a daughter named Diane Forman?" Through a weird coincidence, my mother's ex-husband's name was Bill Forman, and my mother thought they were calling me Diane Forman by mistake. So my mother said, "Yes, that's my daughter." My mother didn't realize they were talking about a different girl. Anyway, the school told my mom that Diane Forman had played hooky that day, so my mom thought I had skipped school. But I hadn't. It was all a big mistake.

When I came in the door from school that day, my mother goes,

"Diane, how was school?" And I said, "Fine." I close the door, and I'm walking past her. Now my mother was famous for wearing stiletto shoes back then, and as I go by her, she hits me right in the head with the pointy heel of her stiletto, and the blood just started flying. I still have a scar on my head from it. Then she grabbed me by my hair and started dragging me down the hallway. I had long, pretty, thick hair. She was five-seven and I was four-eleven, so it was easy for her to overpower me. She snatched me by my hair and dragged me into the bathroom because I was bleeding all over the place.

Somehow, she managed to get ahold of a butcher knife from the kitchen while dragging me down the hall. I don't know how she did that. She was just banging my head everywhere as she dragged me around by my hair. I was like a rag doll. She ended up dragging me into the bathtub and turned on the shower. There was blood everywhere. I'm in the shower with all my school clothes on. My book bag was still on my back. It was crimson red in the shower, blood all up against the wall, all up against the shower. And then she starts trying to cut off my hair with the butcher knife. She's got my hair wrapped around her hand. I'm trying to fight her back. I knew it was fight or die. I couldn't just let her keep at me.

Then, all of a sudden, somebody pulled her up and threw her into the wall. It was Mack. He was yelling and screaming at her, and he pulled her into their bedroom. There was a lot of screaming and hollering. She's yelling, "You're fucking her. You're fucking her." I was thinking, *Come on. You knew this? You knew he was trying to do this to me? You knew?* I went to my knees. *How the hell did I get here? How did I get to this place? How did my life bring me there?* I was so broken.

Then my mother got very, very quiet. He was ranting and raving, and he was threatening to hurt her. Then everything was quiet. At some point, I just went to bed. I had a pounding headache, but they never took me to the hospital. When I was lying on my bed, Mack wouldn't let her anywhere near me.

That night, after she went to work, Mack came into my room when

I was sleeping. He put his hand under the sheet and ran his hand up my leg. I jumped up, startled, and he said, "Shh, I'm not going to hurt you. I'm not going to hurt you." I was tired of fighting, and I wanted to be protected. I really did want to be protected. But then there was that part of me thinking, *My virginity is the only thing I have that's truly mine.* I was just not willing to let him take that away from me.

I wrapped the sheets like a cocoon around me so he couldn't get his hand up my leg. He kept telling me, "Tonight's the night. Tonight's the night," and I knew I couldn't fight him off forever. There's no way I could overpower him, so I thought, *Before I let him do that to me, I'll kill myself.* That night, after he finally left me alone, I climbed out the window onto the fire escape. I climbed over the railing, and I was hanging on that fire escape, off the fifth floor, just hanging there.

I held on to the railing and let my feet go, and I was just holding on by my hands. I could swing back and forth. I was just swaying there, holding that bar. Then I looked down, and I saw this wrought-iron fence below. I thought, *It would be just my luck to get impaled on that fence and end up in a wheelchair for the rest of my damn life. Then I will really be a mess. I'll probably be a vegetable or not able to move my arms and legs for the rest of my life."*

Then this voice in my head said, "Don't do this. Don't do this." I wanted to let go, but something wouldn't let me do it. I call the voice God, I really do. I knew I had to get out of that environment, but I just didn't know how to do it.

I decided not to kill myself that night, but I knew I couldn't get away from Mack. He would still be coming into my room and saying, "Tonight's the night." So I started thinking, *Okay, if he's going to fuck me, I'm going to fuck somebody else first.* I'm know I'm being very graphic with my words, but I was so angry. I refused to let him have my virginity. I was thinking, *You're not going to get my cherry. You're not. I am not going to let you do this to me. Before I let you do this to me, I will do it myself. I will pick somebody else.*

And then, the next day, there's William.

13

I could see a basketball court out the window of my apartment. I used to like to watch this one guy who would play there. I didn't know his name or anything, but I used to like to watch him play. I knew he was older than me.

One day, I was hanging out with my friend Debra. Debra was a very talented person. She used to draw diagrams and all kinds of stuff. She had a lot of plans. She wanted to build buildings and stuff. She ended up being schizophrenic, but she wasn't when I knew her.

Well, anyway, the first time I met William, I was standing outside our building with Debra. We were watching Mary. My mother would let me take her outside to play. We were in a housing complex, and there were two guys standing across the courtyard.

Debra told me how cute one guy was because he was African American with blue eyes. But me and the other fellow locked eyes. He was the one I'd seen on the court. And I felt something strange, like I had never felt before. This was William.

He was a handsome African American guy, and he's just sexy as what. I later learned that he grew up in South Carolina. He even did some modeling before he moved to New York. Here he is in our housing complex, walking around in a silk shirt and cashmere coat. He didn't look like a pimp, nothing like that, but he just loved clothes. He looked as clean as the Board of Health.

William thought I was older. He told me, "You're so pretty. How old are you?" And I answered, "Nineteen," even though I was barely fourteen. When you're abused, you become mature fast. He said he was twenty-two, and he believed I was nineteen. I didn't care that he was older. He was good-looking and a sweet talker. He had that look. He looked at me, and I looked at him, and the next day, we were sleeping together.

Mack had to go to some military thing for two weeks because he was in the Army Reserves, and my mother was working the third shift at the hospital that night. That meant I had the apartment to myself. I got some vodka and orange juice, and I invited William over. I got one of my mom's little teddy negligees and put it on.

I told him I was a virgin, so he promised to go slow. I remember him saying, "I'll just put the head in, just a little, just a little." He was very gentle, but it hurt like hell. Even with the pain, it still felt good to have control over what was happening in my life.

Lord have mercy, though; the sex did hurt me. That thing was painful. It was nothing like I thought it was going to be. I was thinking, *What the hell? This sucks. What's the big hoo-haw about sex?* My mother was always calling me "slut" and "ho" and all kind of names. I remember thinking, *Well, damn. If she's making such a big deal about it, there must be something really good about sex.* It didn't become pleasurable until the third or fourth time. After that, I just wanted to be with William all the time.

At first, I was just a lay to him. I know that, but then he got attached to me and really fell for me. Then he heard my story about what things were like for me at home. One day after we had sex, he saw some fresh bruises on me. He was asking, "What the hell? What is that? What's going on? Diane, who did that to you?" Up until then, I had been making excuses about the marks on me. But this day, I came clean. I told him Mack was beating me and molesting me. I told him the whole story. Everything. He said, "Oh, my God. I want to shoot that motherfucker."

William told his brother what was going on, and his brother said,

"We are going to get her out of there. Tell her to pack her stuff. She's got to go." William told me, "You need to get out of there." I said, "I have nowhere to go. Where am I going to go? I've run away before and been on the streets. I've been in a group home, and they sent me back into the same situation." He promised, "I'll hide you. I'll take care of you. Just meet me tomorrow." And he was true to his word. I ran away, and he took me to his cousin Deborah's house about three blocks from where I lived.

Eventually, Mack found out I was there and tried to knock the door down. Deborah called the police, and the police came and asked her, "Do you have anybody named Diane living here with you?" She lied and said no. The cops couldn't just come in and look around, so they told Mack he had to leave. I told William what happened. I said, "I don't want to get you or Deborah in trouble," but he told me not to worry.

Then, one day, I was walking with William, and all of a sudden, a green Dodge Charger drove up on the sidewalk in front of us. It was Mack driving. He shouted at me, "Get the fuck in the car," but I wasn't going to do it. I wasn't getting in, but I was worried William was going to shoot him because William had a gun. I knew if William shot him, then William would be gone for life.

William tried to talk to Mack. He said, "Look, I love Diane. I want you to know that I want to do right by her. I'm going to go in the military." He was trying to reason with him. But Mack just said, "Fuck you, man." I ended up getting in the car and went with him because I didn't want William to do anything stupid. But I ran away again when I had the chance and returned to William.

Later, Mack came looking for me again. He was driving around the neighborhood in that Charger. William and his brother saw Mack, and they lured him over. Then, they grabbed ahold of him when he got out of the car, and they dragged him somewhere. They put a gun to his head, and William screamed, "If you ever fucking touch Diane again, we'll kill you. You aren't her fucking father." They yelled, "You definitely aren't her father. You're black. Look at her. You aren't her father. If you touch her again, we'll kill you." They had Mack practically pissing himself, and he never touched me again.

14

I must have gotten pregnant one of the first nights I was with William. I finally spoke to him about it and said, "I'm pregnant." He said, "How do you know?" I said, "Because I'm throwing up, and I didn't get my period." I didn't care that I was pregnant. I wanted to be. I wanted my own family. I didn't want to be with my mom and Mack anymore. I was so stupid and naive.

William said, "I'll get you out of here and take care of you." And I said, "You can't get me out of here." He said, "You're nineteen. We can do whatever we want." I said, "No, I'm really fourteen." When I told him how old I really was, he almost died. He said, "You're underage. I'm going to fucking jail." I told him, "No, you're not, because I'm not going to tell them that you're the baby's father." At that time, there was no DNA or stuff to prove who was the father. I would have gone to my grave with that secret because it was my fault. I did tell him I was nineteen when we met.

I didn't know what to do, so I went back home for a bit because I didn't want William to get arrested. But then I ran away again and was back on the streets. I met this kid who was around my age, and he said, "I'll help you." His name was James, and he was another angel. He would let me sneak into his house to take a shower when his mother went to work, and he gave me some of his clothes and stuff. We were about the same size; maybe he was just a little bigger than me. James gave me jeans, a belt, and a T-shirt, and he also fed me.

When his mom went to work, he'd let me come up and hang out in his room with him. For a while, I was staying in his mother's basement whenever I could. I remember there was this drip, drip, drip from the pipes above me when I tried to sleep.

One day, James said, "I know this lady. She's a nun. If you let me, I'll go talk to her about you. You might be able to stay with her." I told him, "See what you can find out because I know I can't go back home." I knew Mack wasn't playing. He was determined to have me, and I was determined not to let him do it. James talked to this nun. She told him to bring me to see her and let her talk to me. So I went.

The place was on 169th Street and the Grand Concourse in the Bronx. It was called GLEE, Group Living Experience, or something like that. Sister Margaret was running it. She never wore nuns' clothes, and she was very sweet. She said, "Diane, we will not let anybody near you, but we have to tell your family that we have you. You have to tell me who you are." I wouldn't give them my name. I said, "No, I'm not telling you who I am. I don't care." And she said, "You have to. But I promise you, you will not have to go with them." I told her, "If you send me back, I swear I will leave as soon as I can. I will be right back out in the streets."

She kept her word, so I stayed with Sister Margaret for a few months. It was a group home. There was a bunch of us, about twelve kids. It was two apartments in a tenement building where the wall had been knocked down. They had intensive counseling, but I would just sit there, curled up in a ball, not saying anything. There was this one counselor named Archie, and he would get in front of me and say, "You know what, Diane? You're going to talk." I just looked up at him and didn't say a word. Then I looked down at my lap again. He said, "I don't care how long you put your head down. When you put your head up, I'll be right here." He really made me trust him, and I opened up a lot. That helped a lot. Those group sessions helped a lot. More angels.

In the group homes, everybody went home for the holidays, and

I was always the odd man out because I definitely wasn't going back to my mom and Mack. Each holiday, somebody would take me home with them. One girl, she was real nice. She was a Muslim. She ended up taking me to a Louis Farrakhan event in a big stadium. They all had these white outfits on. We were eating carrot cake and stuff, and I was the only one that looked like me there. I had no clue what was going on. When I went to other people's houses for Christmas and Thanksgiving, I just felt I didn't belong there. I was grateful they invited me, but I felt like everybody was looking at me with pity. I just felt, *This is not my home. This is not where I belong.*

I stayed in the group home for four months, but it was only a temporary placement, so they wanted to try having me go back home again. I was thinking, *You gotta be freaking kidding me,* and they said, "No, we mean it." There were meetings with them and my mother. She lied and told them the real problem was that I didn't like Mack because he was black. She said I didn't like black people. I said, "That is not true," but they believed what they wanted to believe.

At that point, I was about six months pregnant, so I got sent to Rosalie Hall because I had to have some place to have my baby. Rosalie Hall is a home for unwed mothers on 233rd Street. When I moved in there, I saw this toy stuffed dog in the gift shop. It was a Saint Bernard, and it looked just like the dog in that movie *Beethoven*. I wanted to buy it for my baby because William's middle name was Bernard. It cost $12. Rosalie Hall would give you $3 a week allowance, and I saved my money to buy that dog. What the hell was I thinking? How was I going to take care of a baby? It took me four weeks just to buy a $12 toy.

By this time, William was in Pennsylvania, living at my grandmother Dede's house. He had gotten in trouble in New York, so he needed somewhere else to stay. He had nowhere else to go, so Dede took him in. Dede was really my sister Mary's grandmother, but she let him stay there because she wanted to help me out. One day, Dede called me and told me that William had gone off with a girl named

Sandra. When she told me that, my heart just broke. I decide to get on the train and go see him. I don't remember how I got the money for the fare. Maybe I stole it. I probably did, but I don't know how. Maybe shoplifting.

When I got there, Dede took me to the house where William was staying. I knocked on the door, and Sandra opened it, and she just looked at me. Remember that I'm eight and a half months pregnant. She looks at me and says, "Oh. You must be Diane." Then she opens the door real wide, and who's lying in her bed? William. Just like that, he's pulling the sheets up to cover himself.

I'm staring at him, and my little heart is broken. Sandra is probably twenty-two, twenty-three. She was a very attractive girl. I'm not going to lie, but I was attractive back then too. She's got a bunch of babies on the floor. She was getting high with William, and her kids were literally sleeping on blankets on the floor. It was sad. It was sick. I was so depressed to see William using drugs again.

I stared at William, and then I just turned around and walked out. I went to the park nearby. Dede followed me, but I was yelling, "Just leave me alone." My grandmother went home, but William came running up there after me. I was sitting, looking up at the sun, lying on the grass, and he was saying, "Diane, I had nowhere to stay. Your grandmother kicked me out. I don't care about Sandra. I couldn't give a shit about her, but I have nowhere else to stay."

Well, unfortunately, I know what that feels like. I know what having nowhere to stay feels like. I know what it feels like to be on the streets. He hugged me and held me. He did run after me so that obviously told Sandra something about his feelings for me. There was a connection between him and me. Well, eventually, he went back to Sandra's house. He had to do it because she would have kicked his behind out otherwise, and then he would've been out in the street.

I had no way to help him, so I went back to my grandmother and asked her why she kicked William out. She told me he stole Bill's gun. Remember that Bill was Dede's son and Mary's father. Bill was really angry, and he and William got into a fight. After that went down, of course, she had to kick William out. William told me he didn't steal his gun, but he probably did. He probably did, but I don't know to this day. I never thought to ask him.

15

I went back to Rosalie Hall. I was really hoping I would get into a mother-baby program, but that didn't happen. They thought I was too unpredictable because I ran off to Pennsylvania. Also, I got into a huge fistfight with another girl when I was nine months pregnant. I had two black eyes, and she had two black eyes. I mean, we fought like crazy. I was so angry. I was such an angry person back then. I don't know if she deserved it or not. All I know is that they didn't think I was fit to care for my baby. They told me I wouldn't be able to keep my baby after it was born.

A week later, I went into labor. It was December 8, early in the morning, about 1 a.m. They took me to a Catholic place called Misericordia Hospital in the Bronx. I felt this incredible pain, and I was thinking, *Oh my God!* It was something I never felt like before. And it was a lot of pain. I felt like the people at the hospital were punishing me by how they treated me as I went through all that pain. Nobody came in. Nurses weren't coming in. Nobody, nobody comforted me, nothing. I found myself praying to die. *God, kill me now. Take me now. I cannot take this pain.* Here I am, fourteen years old, the body of a kid, trying to push out this big baby.

It was the most painful thing I had ever been through. They didn't care that I was hurting. One of the nurses actually told me, "Oh, you need to feel the consequences of what you did by getting pregnant." Like I hadn't felt pain before? I knew what the fuck pain feels like. They didn't need to tell me about the pain, but it was like they wanted to punish me for getting pregnant so young. I think they was purposely making me feel so much of the pain so I wouldn't get pregnant again.

The baby ripped me from one end to the other. I had internal stitches. I had hemorrhoids. I'm not kidding you. I was a mess. Back then, there was no epidural. There was none of that. That was hell. I was in agony for six and a half hours. I got a block—they called it a saddle block—toward the last two hours. It paralyzed me from the waist down, and finally, I was able to give birth to my son. I named him Neil, and he came out on the light side. Neil is a very light-skinned African American. He's not real dark, but you can tell he's not white. He looks just like William, only William was very dark, whereas my son was caramel-colored. I wish they'd taken a chance on me for the mother-baby program because I loved my son from the moment I saw him. I would have done anything for him. He was my reason to live once I saw him.

The day after I had Neil, Dede went to Sandra's apartment and told William I had our baby. He came up to New York to the hospital right away. I mean, I wasn't expecting anybody. I gave birth alone. I was shocked to see him. When he came into my room, I realized those emotions were still there. Even though I knew what he was doing was wrong, it doesn't stop the love you have for somebody. After we talked, I got it in my mindset that maybe we could do this after all. He promised to stay off drugs. He made a lot of promises. I had saved up $165. I'll never forget that. And I gave it to him to get us an apartment. Of course, he blew that money to smithereens. That's when I cried and prayed and asked God to take William out of my heart. I knew he was not good for me even though he could be very sweet. He was on drugs, and the drugs had him by the gonads. I had Neil to think about now. We didn't stand a chance living with William.

I think I stayed in the hospital for three days, and then I had to leave. They left Neil in the hospital because he had jaundice. He was very yellow. I tried telling them, "He's just yellow because he's part black." But they said, "No, no, no." And they were explaining that his eyes were yellow, so he had to be in the hospital for a couple of weeks until the jaundice was cured.

My mother never came to the hospital, but she told the social worker that she wanted Neil to come live with her. There's actually a picture of me and my mom the next time I saw her after I had Neil. You can see how sad I look. My mom only came to see me because she was trying to get me to give her my baby, but I told her, "No, I'm not giving you my baby."

I couldn't believe she thought I would do that. She didn't want me as her daughter, but she wanted my baby? Crazy. I told the social worker, "Like hell, she's getting my baby. The only reason she wants the baby is because she thinks maybe it's her husband's baby. She knew he was trying to have sex with me. That's why she wants Neil, but he is not her husband's baby." I told them I'd rather give my baby up for adoption to a stranger than give him to my mother.

The social worker was nice and said, "Sweetie, if you voluntarily give up your son to foster care, the judge will eventually give your son back to you. But you need to do what he tells you to do. We have to go to court." So they gave me a free attorney, and I went to court for a hearing. The judge said, "Do you understand that we are not permanently taking your child from you? He can't live with you now because you are a minor. Do you want your mother to raise your son?" I said, "No way." My mother was in the court, and the judge said, "The biological mother of the child must have a reason that she would rather give her son to foster care than have her own mother take her son."

My lawyer said to the judge, "Diane has been in the foster care system for over a year. She has a case of child sexual abuse against her stepfather, and she doesn't want her son living there." So the judge said if I studied for my diploma and got a trade where I could work, he would reinstate my parental rights when I turned eighteen. Social services would help me get an apartment, so I said, "Okay." And that's what I did.

Sharon and Diane (age fifteen)

16

After Neil was born, William came back to New York, and he stayed around a while. He didn't go back to Pennsylvania, but he was still doing stupid stuff. He was stealing and smoking reefer and getting high, but my own values had changed dramatically, so I wasn't willing to put up with that crap. I was thinking, Okay, I love the hell out of you, but I actually prayed and asked God to take that emotion away from me because I loved my son more. William's life is not what I wanted for Neil. I didn't want that for him.

Then I got pregnant by William again. I know. Crazy. Dumb.

I don't know where I was going in my head back then. I was barely sixteen and love-starved; all I wanted was to be with William. I didn't care about anybody other than him and Neil. I thought about having a second baby, and I was thinking, *I can't have another baby and put it in foster care. I can't do that.* I was begging William to help me, to work with me. "Come on, we gotta get this together." But William's just falling by the wayside. He's drunk or high all the time. He never cheated on me that I knew about other than with Sandra in Pennsylvania, but he was just a freaking hot mess.

When William first came to New York, he was with his brother, a big drug dealer from South Carolina. William did not have a drug problem in the beginning, but then he started messing with his product. That's where the real problems began. I hit my breaking point when I realized he was doing drugs with needles. I saw him do a needle when we were staying at Shorty's house. Shorty was this Hispanic lady, and she lived with a guy named Jimmy. They had in a rundown apartment, and William and me were living in one of the rooms. The walls were really dirty, but I would've done anything to stay with William because that was my heart. He was my heart.

One day, I walked into the room, and I saw him putting a needle in his arm. I was flabbergasted. I think my mouth dropped open. I grabbed his stuff and threw it out the window. He grabbed me and hit me. It was just one time, but one time is too much. I ran out of there, and then he was calling me and calling me, but I was yelling, "No, no, no!" That was it. When he hit me, that was it.

I cried. I mean, I cried and pleaded with God to let me not love him anymore. I just couldn't do that. I had a son now who I needed to focus on. And the court warned me, "If you stay with William, you're not getting your kid back." So what am I gonna do? The long and short of it was that I ended up letting William go, even though I was pregnant by him. He kept calling me and calling me, but I wouldn't take his calls. I started focusing on making sure I was gonna get Neil back.

So here I am, four months pregnant, trying to figure out what to do. I go to social services, and I gotta tell them I'm pregnant. They didn't know. They took me to the infirmary, and a doctor came over, and he said, "Yeah, she's pregnant. And she's very pregnant. She's not just a little pregnant."

From my first pregnancy, I knew I needed the Rhogam shot because I had O-negative blood, which meant I had to worry about this Rh-factor thing. If you don't get that shot, your baby's not protected. Basically, your white blood cells could end up eating the baby's red blood cells, and there's a huge chance of retardation if you don't get the shot. Well, I knew about the shot, but I kind of ignored it. I didn't want to deal with the reality of being pregnant. Knowing that I wasn't taking care of my unborn baby was weighing on me.

Then, they started talking to me about having an abortion.

They took me to St. Vincent's Hospital in Manhattan. I was very upset. I did not want to have an abortion, but I also did not want to have another child in foster care. And I knew my baby might not be healthy because I didn't get that Rhogam shot. I had no prenatal care at all. I was sixteen. And I was thinking, *My God, what am I going to do?* Then I started talking to God, saying, "Well, God, if you don't want me to get this abortion, then you do something about it. You stop it." But nothing happened, so I went through with it.

It was all arranged very quickly. I'm sure that somebody there had to be counseling me, but I don't remember it. Maybe I just blocked it out. I was put into a room at St. Vincent's, and they had to inject this fluid into my abdomen. There was another girl in my room, and she was with a counselor. I was by myself. I feel like that's always my story. I'm by myself. That's the painful part.

Anyway, I fell asleep for a little bit, and then I started cramping. They put these metal things inside me, and I felt a pain, like a really, really bad cramp. I said, "Oh my God, something's happening."

The counselor lady who was with the other girl, she came over to me. I can see her face to this day, and I know this is God's mercy. This is God's mercy, seriously. She was very, very sweet. She said, "Sweetie, you're okay," and I said, "No, something's wrong down there." She asked me, "Can I see how you're doing?" And I said, "Yeah." So she drew the cover back that was over my legs and saw what she saw. I went to lift my head up to look down there, and she gently pushed me back. She said, "Sweetie, you don't want to see this. You don't need to see this."

I thank God for her because she was another angel. Had I looked at what was down there, I would have never gotten over it. It would have wrecked my heart to this day. It still bothers me, and I ask God for forgiveness and thank Him for His grace. It wasn't just a blob. It was a fetus. I'm glad I don't know if it was a girl or a boy.

Next thing, the nurses came in and took it away. Then, the counselor lady sat with me because the other girl was sleeping. She was just stroking my hair, telling me it was going to be okay. I was going to be okay. Eventually, I fell asleep.

I woke up to the sound of screaming. The other girl was screaming her head off because her abortion was happening. She was shouting, "It hurts, it hurts, it hurts!" She's screaming, and I'm just eating breakfast: bacon and eggs. I'm eating my meal like nothing is happening. And this girl looks over at me, and she yells, "Why didn't she scream?" And the counselor lady said, "I don't know. I can't tell you why she didn't go through the pain you went through." Looking back, I think it was partly because I had given birth so recently. But I also believe it was God's mercy and grace that I didn't suffer the same pain that the other girl suffered.

While I was looking at this other girl, I was indifferent to her. I wasn't thinking, *Oh, you poor thing*. I wasn't feeling anything for her. I was going through my own shit, so I was thinking, *You need to just deal with it*. I got a whole lot to deal with myself. At least she had somebody holding her hand.

I wonder about that baby sometimes, but I know in my heart that there was no other decision I could make back then, but it still weighs on me. I think if I saw the fetus, I would've never gotten over it. I would have been traumatized. I don't forgive myself to this day. I know I was only sixteen. I know about the Rh factor, and I know that there was a strong possibility that my baby could've been born deformed with some really bad problems. But I killed my own baby, and that messed with my head for a long time.

17

The judge told me if I wanted to get Neil back, I had to stay away from William because he was on drugs. The judge was right. William was in a bad way, and I knew that we should never get back together. I got my own apartment, and William came by to see me. He bought me a pair of new boots, but I didn't let him stay with me. When I told him he couldn't stay, he took the boots back to sell for drugs. When I heard he did that, I said, "That's why I won't ever take you back," and I broke up with him for good.

There was a big blackout in New York in 1977, and William and some friends broke into a cigarette factory. They stole cartons and cartons of cigarettes and tried to get away. They ran from the police and their car hit a metal subway pillar. William ended up in the hospital, and they had him listed as "black, unknown" because he didn't have any identification on him. People called me and said, "Diane, William's in the hospital. He was in a police chase, but they don't know his name. They won't let anybody see him. But you got his kid, so you can get in there. You need to see if that's really him." I went to the hospital, and it was him, but he was out of his mind. He was calling me "Big Mama," his grandmother's name. I called his mother in South Carolina and told her, "You have to come and get him, or he's going to die up here." She did come up to get him and brought him back to South Carolina.

William got arrested for stealing the cigarettes, but I think they just let it go and gave him a fine. I was out of his life by that time. When he returned to South Carolina, he hooked up with a married woman who he ended up marrying. He never came back to New York. She put up with the drugs and drinking, tolerating it all. He ended up screwing a bus driver behind her back. I heard all about this stuff from friends who still stayed in touch with him. He and his wife ended up doing a lot of fighting and arguing. He was always going to his mother's house. It was all very dysfunctional. He was drinking, getting high. I just didn't want any part of that.

18

I worked some odd jobs, but mainly, I would steal to survive. I stole up until I turned eighteen. I thought there was nothing the cops could really do to me until I turned eighteen, so I would steal stuff from Alexander's. Anybody who's my age will know what Alexander's is. Anybody that's young won't have a clue, but it's like a nice Kmart.

I would go to Alexander's wearing a really long coat. I'd put stuff across my arm and under my coat. I took some stuff in the back in the dressing rooms. I'd go in there and put on the new clothes. Back then, they didn't have those plastic sensors. They had none of that. After I would steal that stuff, then I would go and sell it. Sometimes people would give me their orders in advance. "I want size ten. I want this. I want that." I was making a lot of money, and sometimes I was staying in hotels with my friends.

Anyway, the security guards at the store caught me one day, and I actually got arrested. The police tried to get me to go home to my mother, but I was saying, "No, I'm not going back there. Absolutely not." I told them, "If you leave me there, I will be out the door as soon as you leave." So they decided to put me in handcuffs, and they took me up to the Kennedy Home on Stillwell Avenue near Pelham Parkway. I think 1770 Stillwell Avenue was the address. It's a group home for teenage girls. We passed by Jacobi Hospital on the way there. On the other side of Pelham Parkway was an above-ground subway station. They had put me in handcuffs because I was fighting.

I was so combative. When we got to the Kennedy Home, they took the handcuffs off. Somebody met me at the gate. As I walked in, the counselor said, "Don't be scared. It's okay. Nobody's going to hurt you. It's okay."

There were no Puerto Ricans in the Kennedy Home at the time, so I was the only one that looked like me. I could sense the tension in the air right from the start, like somebody was going to try to hurt me. But this one girl named Kate befriended me. She was very butchy in stature. She dressed like a boy and had an Afro. Half her hair was gone where she had a burn scar, so she was part bald. She told me her mother had put her head on the radiator and burned her when she was a kid. Her mom scalded her head so bad that no hair could ever grow there. She would always wear a cap to cover it up. It was one of those flat caps like old Englishmen with a pipe would wear.

Well, Kate befriended me. Her advice was to act crazy around the other girls to help protect myself. She also said, "You going to have to fight one of the big girls here. You need to prove yourself." These big girls were six-foot easy, and I was probably four-eleven. But I did it. There were these grapefruits in the cafeteria, so I took a couple and threw them at one of the biggest girls. Then I ran. I acted as crazy as I could. One day, I grabbed a bunch of knives and threatened some of the girls. It took the staff a while to get the knives away from me.

Later, Kate told me, "Those girls are gonna come get you in the nighttime. They want revenge." I said, "What am I gonna do?" She went to her locker and got the iron that she pressed her clothes with. She said, "Plug this in and put it under your bed. When they come for you, hit the first person you can with it." That's what I did. One of them came over to my bed, and she stabbed me in the arm with a knife. I still got the scar. After that, I hit her right on her face with the iron and burned her bad. Since I was attacked first, I wasn't charged. Nobody ever touched me ever again after that. I don't think I would have survived there without Kate. Another angel.

We were all angry kids at the Kennedy Home. We would throw

bottles of piss at the counselors. We did that sometimes. We'd take the metal beds, back them against the door, and play spades. We threw mattresses out of windows and stuff like that.

One day, we got a spoiled kid in the Kennedy Home. She was a brat and always calling her mother a bitch and other stuff. Her momma was always up in the office crying about her daughter. She'd be bringing her $300 worth of stuff each time. We would steal this girl's stuff and beat the crap out of her. We told her, "Better run back home." That girl's name was Julie, I'll never forget. She ran back home. Her mother came and got her. She didn't belong there.

But nobody messed with Kate. She was tough. She was very tough. She was my BFF. Yes, she was. She used to write lovely poems. She was very, very talented at poetry, but nobody really liked her because she was so butch. She was gay. Back then, in the '70s, it was not like it is now when it comes to how gay people are treated.

Kate's mother was also gay, and one day, Kate went home for her mom's birthday. While she was there, her mother's girlfriend tried to have sex with Kate. She wanted them to do ménage à trois or something like that. Kate was really upset by it. She called me on her way back to the Kennedy Home. She said, "I'm going to get a forty-ounce." That's a forty-ounce bottle of beer, and she said, "We are going to drink." I said, "Well, go get the forty-ounce, and we'll just get drunk." I said, "We can't go anywhere else worse than here. We can't go any farther down. We are at the bottom. We might as well get drunk."

So I'm waiting and waiting for Kate to come back with the beer, and it starts getting late, but there's still no sign of her. Then I hear the front doors open and close, the clanging of metal doors. Then I hear some talking and giving a description, "Afro, no hair on one side," and I go down there. I yell, "What's going on?" The counselor says, "We think Kate got hit by a car."

I bolted out of there and started running down the highway toward the hospital. The highway had cars coming this way and that way, and there was a big section of grass down the middle. It was very wide and had trees and everything. I was just running straight down the highway, barefoot all the way to the hospital. I get up there and find out that Kate's been put on life support. She died within twenty-four hours. It turns out that while she was walking back to the Kennedy Home, the hat she always wore had blown off her head into traffic. When she ran to get it back, she got hit by a car.

When I returned to the Kennedy Home, I just lied on my bed. It was a very tough time for me because nobody really liked Kate at the Kennedy Home. They really didn't like me either, but I do remember that they all apologized to me after she died. They knew Kate and I were close, so they showed me some sympathy.

I just spent the night thinking about Kate. I realized that just a few hours earlier, I was saying to her, "We're at the bottom. There's nowhere else to go." And then the thought came into my head: *Living here is not the real bottom. You can end up six feet under.* That was one of those pivotal moments in my life that showed me that no matter how bad things are, they can actually get worse. You could go six feet under.

Diane's ID badge from the Kennedy Home

19

When I turned seventeen, Neil was still in foster care, and I was living at the Kennedy Home. I went to work as a nurse's aide at Bird S. Coler Hospital on Wards Island, a nursing home for old people. I had to take the train and then a bus to get there, and sometimes I had to wait for a long time. This neighborhood must have been Hookerville, where all the hookers are, because this one girl said to me, "You need to move on. This is my corner." I told her, "You can have it. I'm not interested in that stuff."

If I worked late, I would take a cab back to Kennedy Home. Sometimes the drivers would pull out their dicks while we were stopped at the red light. They'd be saying, "Come and sit in the front. I'll give you a free ride." As soon as that light turned green, I jumped out. It's amazing that nothing really bad happened to me. I know I had to have guardian angels around me to protect me from all the stuff I experienced.

When I went to work at Bird S. Coler, there was this one bed with a curtain drawn around it all the time. I heard there was this young guy in there behind the curtain. Everybody else in the hospital was senior citizens, and all you could smell was poop and urine. I was thinking the young guy in this bed must really be crazy.

One night, while eating in the cafeteria, this guy in a wheelchair rolled up next to me. He goes, "Hi. I'm Sammy," and I said, "All right, Sammy, but I don't know you, so why are you talking to me?" He said,

"Yeah, you do. I'm the one in the bed behind the curtain where you always try to look." I said, "That's you?" He said, "Yeah, I gotta draw my curtain all the time. I can't deal with all that shit going on around me." I asked him, "What are you doing in here?" He said, "I got shot." I said, "You got shot?" He said, "Yeah. Two years ago."

He said that his mother had bought his father a shotgun for Christmas. His father got drunk and tried to shoot his mother. Sammy jumped in front of his mother and took the bullets. He ended up with a colostomy bag and was paralyzed from the waist down. He was living at the hospital because his mother lived in a fifth-floor apartment, and there was no way for Sammy to walk up the stairs to her place.

This was another good lesson. As I looked at Sammy, I thought, *No matter how bad my life is, other people have it worse.* This guy's my age, stuck in a nursing home hospital. What a horrible place for a kid. His mom has no insurance, and he's too young to be placed in an apartment by himself. They had to keep him at the hospital until he turned eighteen and could get Section 8 housing to have his own place. Since he couldn't get around, I decided to help him out. I took it upon myself to be his legs. I'd call people, like social workers, to help him get on waiting lists for resources and things like that.

My heart went out to him, and I even fell in love with him. At least, I thought I did. But there was never any actual sex between us because he was paralyzed. I mean, I'd sit on him. He'd roll around, and I'd sit on his lap. We'd be rolling around. We'd be down by the water all night long, talking and sleeping outside.

I got fired for fraternizing with the patients, but I didn't care. I mean, I loved him. I really did. But the truth of the matter was that I wanted to have more kids one day, and I wanted to have sex. As much as I loved him, that was never going to happen between him and me. I tried to be his friend as much as I could, but he got angry that I wanted to stay just friends. I told him, "I have a son, and I want to be your friend, but I can't do this kind of relationship." It was a huge responsibility because he needed a lot of care. He had a colostomy. He had a Foley catheter. That was a lot.

But I did end up helping him get his own apartment when he turned eighteen, and I did go see him. Every Christmas, I made sure I always contacted him and went to see him. His family, they didn't treat him well. Everybody wanted him for his disability check. It was just very, very sad. I knew these people were using him, but there was nothing I could do about it because Sammy really wanted that human connection. His mother had fourteen kids, and they all just took advantage of him. They would stay at his house because they knew he had free rent. So his house was always packed with people.

I used to spend the night with him and hang out with him. But then he let all these different people move in, and they were drinking. The lesson I learned from Sammy was that no matter how hard my life was, I have my legs. I could walk away from the situation. Sammy could not. He was a dear friend to me. My heart went out to him because everything for him was a struggle. You had to lift Sammy into a cab. You had to carry him up four flights of stairs. Sammy couldn't do anything, and his legs were badly mangled.

In a way, I thought of Sammy as one of my angels, even though I was protecting him more than he was protecting me. I learned a lot about caring for another person by spending time with him, and that's an important life lesson.

Sammy ended up getting with a girl who already had twin sons. Sammy wanted love and belonging, and she gave him that. I think she let him eat her vagina. I'm not trying to be gross. That's what he told me he would do to her. He would get her off, stuff like that. He told me it made him feel like a man. I said, "I'm happy for you. I really am."

One day, I called him. "Hey. I haven't heard from you. How are you doing?" He told me he didn't think he was going to live much longer. He was in his twenties, so I said, "You'll be fine. You'll be fine." I used to see him at Christmas, but I didn't that year. When I reached out the following Christmas, I found out he died. He'd been dead nearly a year. That was a big regret. I think Sammy knew he was dying the last time we talked, but I didn't listen to him. I should've known he was going to die because he was so torn up from the waist down.

So now, when people tell me something like that, oh, I listen. I listen.

20

Around this time, I started trying to get serious about school. That was one of the requirements the judge made for me to get Neil back. I had to get my high school diploma.

It was hard. I started out going to Roosevelt High School, but it was a mess. There were a lot of gangs back then, and when we were in the cafeteria, they would open the window and bring in weapons with a string or whatever. I was sitting in the cafeteria one day, and I watched this one kid come after another kid with a chain. He started beating the hell out of him. After that, I never went back to Roosevelt again. Then, I was put in this school called West Side High. It was an experimental school with an open concept or whatever they call it. That didn't really work for me either, so now I'm thinking that I'm never gonna get Neil back. It's gonna take too long.

Then they told me about the GED. This is the equivalent of a high school diploma, but you just have to take one big test. I studied hard and worked with tutors, but I failed the GED two times. I decided to take it for the third time, but I was really struggling with the math section. I had a real issue with math because of Mack beating the crap out of me, hitting me every time I got a math problem wrong. I still have a thing about math. Well, guess what? If I show you my GED test results, you will see my highest grade is a 50-something in math. Everything else is 33, 34.

I'll tell you what happened. While I was taking the test, somebody came by behind me and started pointing at the right answers. I just took that pencil and started filling them in where she pointed. It was this teacher, and she knew I was trying hard to get my son back. She knew I was in there every day—hours, hours, hours of studying. She just couldn't take seeing my struggle like that anymore. I was on the last page of the booklet, and she just started pointing at the answers. Even with that help, I was completely discouraged. I actually took the test book and threw it in the trash because I thought there was no way I could pass. I had just given up on myself.

But all of a sudden, a month later, everyone's saying, "Congratulations!" I'm wondering, *What are you talking about?* And they tell me, "You passed the GED." I can't believe it. Then I looked at the math scores, and I realized it was because that teacher gave me those last ten answers. It made all the difference. She was another angel in my life. Should I have cheated? Well, no, I shouldn't have. But I would've guessed at the answers anyway. Would I have passed? Only God knows. But I did pass.

I remember that I called my mother that day because I was all excited to tell her that I passed. You know, it's funny because I haven't thought about this memory in years. When I called her to tell her that I graduated, I got nothing. Nothing. No congratulations. Nothing. Nothing. My heart just broke a little more. There were other people who were really, really happy for me. But it's not the same. She was my mom, and despite everything that happened, I wanted her to be proud of me. But my news just didn't register. Didn't ring a bell. There was no nothing. That hurt. That hurt, but it was a lot to be thankful for because I passed. And that meant getting my son back.

21

While I was living in the Kennedy Home, there was a counselor named Hopper. One night, he said to me, "Diane, come into my office." It was late at night. I go into his office, and he's saying to me, "Where have you been?" because I'd been staying out later than I should. I say, "Oh, here, there, and everywhere." He says, "If you keep acting this way, they're going to send you upstate to a more locked-down place. That's what they're going to do." I looked at him, and I said, "Hopper, you're not going to let them do that to me." I was a flirt. I was trying to be very cute.

I said, "Hopper, you're not really going to let them do that to me, are you? I'm not bothering anybody. I'm not hurting anybody. I'm just trying to get to eighteen and get the fuck out of here. You got these girls here trying to hurt me and do all kinds of stuff. I can't stand this life. This place is chaos." Suddenly, he gives me this look and says, "Close the door." So I closed the door of his office behind me.

Well, as soon as the door was closed, that man pressed himself up against me. I thought, *No, this can't be happening*. I wasn't afraid because I have to admit I had feelings for him. Even though he was much, much older than me. William was seven years older than me, but Hopper was thirty-five, almost twenty years older.

All of a sudden, he's holding me and telling me, "I missed you. I can't let you do this anymore. You can't do this." He started kissing me. I'm thinking. *Okay, this is not happening*. But on one level, I'm glad it's happening because William had really turned to drugs, and I knew I could not be with him anymore because I now had a son in foster care. I had prayed and asked God to take away my intimate feelings for William, but I still loved him because he was Neil's father. I knew it was a no-hope situation because William was too far gone.

So, that night, Hopper ends up opening up another room. We end up doing it right there on the floor. Yes, we did. It felt so good just having somebody holding me, telling me they loved me. Of course, when I think about it nowadays, it's different. Now I think, *How dare you do that to me? Because I was a kid, and you're the head counselor.* I wish I could go back in time and press charges. I would have owned that place.

Later, he invited me to come to his house. He gave me money. He said, "Okay, you know I'm going to work tonight, but I want you to stay here." He gave me his key. I was in his house for three, four, five days. He taught me things about sex that I had no clue about. He went downstairs on me, and I was thinking, *Oh, my God!* All I knew from William was missionary. I'm a kid. Hopper did things to me that just rocked my world.

I loved him. I just literally fell head over heels for him, but I kept our secret. I wouldn't do anything to let anybody else know what was going on, but I got mad at him sometimes. I threw milk at him one time because I thought he was looking at another girl at the Kennedy Home or trying to ignore me. I thought, *You're not getting away with that.* I'd threaten to tell, but I never did. There were a lot of things going on in that group home that should not have gone on. A lot of sex was going on with the counselors, but I never called him out. I never told anybody.

Later that year, they shut down the Kennedy Home because of all the messed-up stuff going on there. At that point, I was seventeen years old, and the judge declared that I was an emancipated minor because I had a kid of my own and had gotten my GED. Since they were shutting down the Kennedy Home, the judge put me on welfare, and I was able to get my own place.

Once I got my own place, Hopper would come over to stay with me some nights. How crazy is that? But I was very needy. I was telling him, "Hold me, hold me, hold me." I was a kid. I was still really needy. Later, Hopper met this other woman who was more independent and knew who she was. She had her own car. She had a good job. So Hopper left me for her. I knew I could take him down. I could go to the authorities and tell them what he had done, but I didn't have the heart to do that.

During this time, I decided to bring Neil to South Carolina to see William because I heard he was doing well down there. I also wanted Neil to meet his grandmother, William's mother. When we talked on the phone, she would say to me, "Why don't you bring Neil down to visit? Bring my baby down." So, I brought Neil to South Carolina. During my visit, William and I ended up in a hotel room because a piece of me still loved William to death, and he wasn't married at the time. He was promising me all this stuff.

But I was actually more in love with Hopper then. I still liked William, but I was more infatuated with Hopper. I told William, "We aren't going to get back together even though we did have a fling at the hotel." That fling told me that spark was gone. We did have sex, but it was more mechanical. It wasn't the feelings that you're supposed to have when you make love to somebody. That just wasn't there for me. It might have been there for him, but it wasn't there for me anymore.

William's family lived in the projects in downtown Charleston, and everybody in the projects loved William. While I'm there visiting, he's taking Neil around and telling people, "This is my kid," and they're saying, "Oh! He's cute." We went to a swimming pool under the Cooper River Bridge one time. I've got pictures of that. Everybody was okay with me and tolerant of us as long as we were in William's neighborhood. But as soon as we went into the white areas of town, look out. Some white guys in a pickup truck started throwing tomatoes at us because I was white and he was black. They were calling me "nigger lover" and stuff like that. After that, I told William, "I can't stay down here. This is not good. I'm heading back to New York."

I was really tired of William's immaturity, and now I'm used to Hopper, who's much older and more established. I'm thinking, *I know what I'm doing*, but I didn't know nothing. When you're that age, you think you know everything, but you don't. I didn't realize that Hopper was just using me. I was not getting it at all.

Hopper and I didn't speak for a year, and then, one day, he called me out of the blue. He ended up coming by and took me to his house. We resume having sex. The relationship is casual, whatever. I just wanted to have sex with him. Then I got pregnant. Dumb, I know. When I told him I was pregnant, I didn't know what to expect. He threw me out of his house! He literally physically grabbed me and threw me out of his house. I'm banging on his door, and I'm crying. His neighbor is yelling, "Hopper, what's going on?" And I'm yelling, "Open the door." But he never let me back in.

That was tough. He had always told me that his mother was prejudiced because he was black and I was white. He told me that she would not accept having a white girl have a baby by him. He insisted that she was not having that. I don't know if this was true or why he didn't want to be with me. I don't know if he got scared because he knew I was very young and all this could come out in the wash. He could end up going to jail. I don't know what his real motivation was for it. I left his place, and I cried.

Anyway, I decided to get an abortion. In one way, I wanted to keep the baby, but it made no sense. He didn't want it. I was thinking, *I already got a kid. How am I going to have another kid? I don't even have my one kid full-time right now.*

Six months later, Hopper comes around again, and we start fooling around. Again, I get pregnant. And he throws me out. He had some other woman in there when I went to tell him I was pregnant. When I saw her, I was asking, "Who is that, Hopper?" And he said,

"You got to leave," and I said, "Well, I'm pregnant," and the other girl is shouting, "She's pregnant?" And he's yelling at her and pushing me out the door. I'm screaming, "Why the fuck did you come back to me? Why did you let this happen? I got pregnant, but you could have did something yourself to stop that if you didn't want no babies."

I felt like I had no choice but to get another abortion. I thought, *I just can't have another baby on my own. I can't do this.* So, that was my third abortion.

I want you to understand that I am not proud of this. All these abortions happened before I was twenty-one. I was a hot mess. I didn't love me, not at all. And I regret to this day the taking of an unborn life like that. I continue to ask God for his forgiveness.

After that, it was truly over for Hopper and me. I didn't deal with him again.

I did see him one more time. He ended up marrying one of my best friends, believe it or not. It was a couple of years later. She told me that she had fell in love with him, and she asked how I felt because she knew I used to date him. I said, "I'm fine with it," but she really didn't give a damn what I thought. Hopper was attracted to people that were self-confident and just didn't care. This woman had two kids by two different men, and he accepted her two kids and had three more with her. Those kids would piss on his furniture and everything, and he would just put up with it.

He became a police officer, believe it or not. When I saw him years later, I told him, "You really took advantage of me." And you know what he told me? "Somebody had to teach you." I said to myself, *You dirty son of a bitch!* Now that I'm in my fifties, I get so mad when I think about how he treated me. After he threw me out, I could have killed myself. I could have hurt myself. I had two abortions because of him. I regret that. I had no idea what I was doing to myself and to my unborn fetuses. I just wanted somebody to love me. He told me he loved me, and I believed him, but sex is not love. These kids today, that's what they think. They think sex is love, and it's not.

22

After I moved out of the Kennedy Home, they put me on public assistance. I had a social worker named Bryan who had to sign all my papers for my checks. I was so young that I didn't know how to manage my money, and there was never enough. There were never enough food stamps to get you through the month. I tried to pick up odd jobs here and there, but every time I picked up an odd job, they cut my benefits. Every time I turned around, I didn't have money for rent.

At one point, I went to work at a restaurant, and Michael was the manager. I liked him, but he had a girlfriend. At the time, I was still pissed off because that other girl had taken Hopper away from me, so I wanted to see if I could do the same thing with Michael. And I did. He left his girlfriend for me. Stupid. We do dumb things when we're young. But anyway, he and I got along really well, but he was very much a mama's boy. He had to be home by a certain time, and I'm used to having more freedom since I had my own apartment. He's telling me he's got to leave by one o'clock in the morning to get back to his mother's house. And I'm like, *The hell with this shit.*

When I fell short and couldn't pay the rent, I'd just end up moving to another place and then another place. At the time, it was really easy to find new places. You just called the superintendent of the building. They'd put you in touch with the landlord, and then you'd go talk to the landlord. As long as you could come up with the deposit, they didn't care. These were slum buildings. They weren't affluent buildings. They were walk-up brownstone tenements. You open the door, and you immediately see cockroaches running. You might even see a little mouse dropping here or there. They don't paint the apartment before you move in, and the floors are just nasty. But when the choice is that or living on the streets, what are you going to do? I'd just take one room and try to fix it up, make it as cozy as possible. I would ignore the rest of the place.

I had a mattress, a TV stand, and a TV, and I carried my clothes in garbage bags. I didn't have dressers or anything like that. I couldn't afford it. It was easy to move that way. In the middle of the night, my friends and I would pack my stuff, and we'd move to the next place. That went on for almost three years, just moving from place to place, staying there for as long as you can stay there. You figure out when they're going to kick you out, so you move before they can kick you out.

When you have nobody, survival is your basic need. I've been on the street. I've slept in basements. I've stolen from supermarkets. Walking around, eating stuff as I went, and then I'd run out. What are you going to do? Arrest me? At least I would have a place to sleep. That's sad when you think, *Okay, arrest me. At least I have a place to sleep and something to eat.* But that's what it came down to. It was crazy.

I never used drugs. I drank a little bit of alcohol, just had a beer or whatever. I never did any of that stupid stuff. I never smoked cigarettes, and I refused to be a prostitute because that's what my mother was when she was younger. I was thinking, *I'm not going to do that. I'll rob a bank before I do that. I'll never sell my body.*

Well, as we're speaking now, I have to admit that's not exactly true. There was this guy named Alan. Alan loved me. God, that man was crazy about me, but I couldn't stand him. I had no feelings for him whatsoever. He always wanted to take me out, but I was uninterested. Well, I couldn't pay my light bill one month. It was wintertime, and I was thinking, *I got to pay this light bill, or I'm going to freeze to death.* Anyway, Alan called me, and I let him come over and have sex with me. He gave me money for my light bill. Afterwards, I was in the shower crying, because I had always had sex with who I wanted to have sex with. I had never had sex with somebody because I needed to pay a bill. Even though Alan liked me—and I know he liked me—I didn't like him like that. I cried that night, and I said to myself, *God, I am never going to let this happen again.*

23

Even though Neil was living with the foster family, I was allowed short visits with him. When he was about one year old, I noticed that the nipple on his bottle was slit open. I said, "My God, this milk is coming out too fast." I had babysat kids, so I knew that you shouldn't do that. His foster mom was also giving him cereal when he was four months old, so my son got very chubby very quickly.

At the time, I did not know that foster parents are given money to take care of kids. I thought this was just some person who randomly wanted to help my son. So I busted my behind working different jobs to buy him clothes and do all kinds of stuff. Nobody—not one time—told me, "Diane, the foster mom gets money to do all this stuff"—nobody. They just accepted what I bought him. I guess the social workers figured I wanted to do it, so why stop me?

I started the process of getting Neil back from foster care when he was two. The problem was, I had no parenting skills. When I brought him to my apartment, Neil was crying his eyes out. I had automatically assumed he would love me because I'm his mother. Well, my son couldn't stand me. He didn't know me because he had spent all his time with the foster family. I was pulling my hair out because he wouldn't stop crying.

It got to the point where I wanted to take my son by the feet and slam him against the wall. I literally wanted to do it because I couldn't take him crying anymore. I called my social worker, Bryan, and I said,

"Bryan, I'm afraid I'm going to hurt Neil." Bryan was asking, "What's going on?" And I said, "He's screaming. I can't take it. I can't take it." He's saying, "Diane, calm down." He sent a social worker over to my house, and she tried to get Neil to calm down. She managed to get him calmed down, and she taught me a couple of techniques to do with him. But as soon as she left, he started up again.

Later, I found a letter from his foster mother. Her name was Anna, and she tucked the letter inside Neil's suitcase. It said, "Please call me. I'd love to see Neil again, if you let me." So I called her, she came over, and he stopped crying. She held him, and he was just in pig heaven. Seeing how happy Neil was with her brought back memories of when I was taken away from Carolyn Hart. I was forced to leave my family in England, and I remembered how painful that was.

I thought, *I can't do that to Neil. Taking him away from her so quick wasn't right.* I told Anna, "Look, this has got to be between you and me." I said, "I have the right to do whatever I want with my son. He's my son. I'm willing to let you take him for a while." She was begging, "Please let me take him. Let me bring him back to you a little bit at a time." I agreed that was probably the best for him. I told her, "Don't mess with me. I will be fair to you. I can see that my son loves you, but don't ever think that I don't love him—because I do. And eventually, he's going to come back to me all the time." And she said, "Yes! Oh, yes."

At the time, I didn't know that she was putting horrible things in Neil's head. During our short visits, as he got older, he would cry all the time. I'd be asking, "Why are you crying? You're only here visiting for just a couple of days." I didn't realize that his foster mother had been telling him, "Your mom is going to spank you. She's going to do this to you. She's going to do that." I had no clue. My son told me this stuff when he was older. I had no clue at the time. It took years before I realized how bad the situation was. Wait until you hear about that part.

24

After I got my GED, I decided I wanted to keep learning. I went and enrolled in some classes at Hunter College, but I didn't know anything about academic advising or any of that. They just let me register for whatever classes I wanted. In my first semester, there were hundreds of students in this big auditorium-type class, and I felt so stupid. I couldn't keep up with what the professor was saying. It was way over my head. I left pretty quick, and I didn't go back to college. I felt so dumb.

At the time, I'm working two part-time jobs in fast-food restaurants. I was using somebody else's Social Security card, working under their name so I could continue getting welfare. I was doing pretty good for myself that way.

One day, I'm talking to my friend at work about what happened at Hunter. She was going to a different college, and I told her, "You must be really smart. I was too dumb to make it into college." She said, "Diane, there's nothing dumb about you." I said, "Girl, please. I went to Hunter College and failed." She said, "Well, what did you take?" And I said it was some 400-level class.

She said, "Diane, you took a 400-level class? Do you know what you're saying?" And I said, "No, what am I saying?" She said, "Diane, you've got to take 100-level before you get to 400—it's 100, 200, 300. You took a class you had no business taking." She took me back to Hunter College. They looked at my GED and told us, "You need to go to a community college and take this test. When you take this test, they're going to place you in the right classes." Well, when I took the test, I was in remedial math, remedial English, and remedial reading—because I had never went to high school.

I must have spent a year and a half just taking remedial courses, maybe even two years. I went to Bronx Community College from 1988 to 1989. It was a two-year college. I ended up with two degrees, an associates in elementary education and an associates in human services. I also had enough credits for an associates in psychology. I had learned to be a full-time student, while still making a lot of money off the government.

I had learned to scam the government. I was thinking, *I'll just jump from one degree to another degree.* I was also getting welfare. I could get all my welfare services, and I could get all my Pell grants. I did college work-study. It was a good deal for me, and I still got food stamps. I was in school, but I had become welfare-dependent.

Diane, age 21

25

When I was at the Kennedy Home, there was a girl named Paula who was having sex with another senior counselor named Mike. This was going on at the same time that I was having sex with Hopper. Paula ended up living with Mike for a while, but then Mike went back to his wife. Paula was like six feet tall, a very, very pretty African American girl. At that point, she had nowhere to go, so I let her move in with me. When she moved in with me, I sometimes had Neil on the weekends. And so I gave her the bedroom because I had a really gigantic living area. The apartment was really nice. It was a step up for me. I had room for a full-sized bed and all his toys. I told Paula she could stay with me if she watched Neil while I worked, and she was okay with that.

One day, I get a call from her while I'm at work. She says, "Diane, they robbed us." I'm saying, "Are you serious?" And she says, "Yeah, girl. You've got to get back here. You got to get back quick." I get back there, and we call the police. The apartment is a mess. It was Christmas, and they took all my gifts. They stole my son's Star Trek stuff. Star Trek was the big thing back then. They took all his Star Trek stuff and his stuffed puppy. I mean, that was all gone. Pictures all smashed. Couches were ripped open. I'm thinking, *Damn, is someone mad at me?* Like okay, you robbed me, but why do so much damage? I mean, I only had cheap furniture. It was one of those first living room sets you buy from the discount store. The tables were smashed.

A few weeks later, I was walking by the apartment where I knew Paula's sister lived. When I walked by their place, I saw a ceramic duck in their window. I immediately realized that it was the same one my grandmother Dede gave me years ago. It was definitely the same ceramic duck that was in my house, and it was stolen that day. At that point, I realized that Paula must have had something to do with the robbery. I didn't say anything to her, but I went back to the police.

This time, they asked me more questions, like whose stuff was in the bedroom. I said that's mostly Paula's stuff. And they said, "And whose stuff was in that closet?" I said, "That's my stuff." They said, "Well, you see how your stuff was all gone? And a lot of her stuff was still here? Sweetie, this was an inside job." I said, "But why did she tear up my house like this?" They said, "I guess she was trying to throw you off so you wouldn't suspect her." But that didn't really make sense to me.

Finally, I realized what had happened. I used to get food stamps, and they came in these little booklets. Being that I worked in restaurants, I would feed my son with food from the job. I'd buy what food he needed from the store, but it wasn't much because he wasn't with me all the time. Paula knew I had saved up $700 worth of food stamps, but she didn't know that I carried them with me everywhere I went. That's what she was looking for that day. She was looking for my food stamps.

When I realized what happened, I said to myself, "Okay, bitch. Okay. We'll fight fire with fire." Now I'm angry. Long story short, I called the landlord and told him what happened. He said, "I'll tell you what I'll do. I will find you another apartment. Give me a couple of weeks."

Once the landlord got me the new place, he sent the super to change the locks at the old apartment. Then he got the police to put all Paula's stuff out on the street. He made it clear she couldn't stay there anymore, so she ended up on the street. I didn't feel bad for her at all. She had to go live with her sister or whatever. She deserved it.

26

At one point, I ended up living with my friend, Lucy. I was nervous after Paula, but she was much better to live with. Lucy lost her own place, so she came and stayed with me. Lucy worked for the ASPCA and got me a weekend job there, but I was scared to death of the animals. I stood on top of the cages while Lucy cleaned them. I was scared of the big pit bulls and German shepherds and stuff. The boss ended up firing me because I couldn't do the work. I shouted at her, "You're firing me?" I turned her desk over. I was such an angry kid back in them days.

Well, Lucy was still working there, and I was working other jobs. One day, she said, "Diane, I got this guy I want you to meet." I said, "Why? Who?" And she goes, "His name is Will." I said, "No, I don't want to meet another guy named William. No, no, no." She goes, "Well, he likes me, but I don't like black guys, so I told him about you because I know you like black guys."

Will also worked for the SPCA, but he was an animal tech. He went out on calls and picked up stray animals. So, I meet him, and he's got a brand-new car. I'm thinking, *Hmmm*. But I don't like him like that much at first. We go to the Botanical Gardens, and somehow, I made him spend $150 on me. I don't know on what. He had a $300-a-week job, and that was pretty good money. My rent was $150 a month, so I was thinking, *Maybe this guy is okay.*

I didn't fall in love right away with the second William. Let me call him "Will" so you don't get confused with the first William. At first, I ended up falling in love with Will's family. His family had a beautiful house in Queens, and they looked like *The Waltons*, the African American Waltons. Grandma and Grandpa lived there, and a tenant lived in the basement. What I didn't know was there was a major history of alcohol abuse in that home. I also come to find out that the lady living in the basement was actually having sex with Will's father. His mother didn't have sex with him anymore because she had some disease that makes sex painful, so she put up with the girlfriend in the basement.

Not exactly the Waltons, I guess.

Will ended up growing on me because he used to make me laugh. But he was doing drugs, and I just ignored the warning signs. You would have thought I learned my lesson after what happened with the first William. Will had a brand-new car, so I thought life was still good. But then I got pregnant, and things had to change. I decided to have the baby, but I told him he needed to get his act together. He was thinking about going into the military, and I said, "Okay, I'll marry you if you go into the military." He agrees at first, but then he changes his mind. I said, "Then I'm not marrying you because I'm not going back to living on the street. You need to get serious and clean up your act. I can't take chances now that I'm going to have two kids."

At that point, I was a welfare mom. I was young, but I knew what living on the streets felt like. I already had one child living part-time in foster care. So I said to Will, "You know what? I will continue to get welfare, go to school, and do everything they tell me to do. I'm not getting off welfare unless you marry me and go into the military."

Well, he goes into the military for a while, and I give birth to my daughter. But then Will has an affair with this girl named Linda. When I found out about it, I was thinking, *Okay, fuck you*. Then he decides he's not going to come back to me, and instead he wants to go back home and live with his parents. But his dad chewed him out, saying, "Are you out of your mind? Get the hell out of my house. You need to go back to Diane and your daughter."

His father put him out. He said, "You made a baby with that girl, and now you want to be with somebody else? No way. You're twenty-one. Get out." At that point, Will's father actually came to my rescue and bought me a baby crib. Will's father's name was Daniel, and I named my daughter, Danielle, after him. He loved that baby. For a year, his father really helped me with the baby.

He would buy my daughter anything, do anything for me, do anything for her. He was a wonderful man. He tried to have sex with me too. I was thinking, *You know what? You aren't having sex with me because I love your wife, and I would never do that to her.*

There are certain things that I draw the line against. That was one of them. I did a lot of dirt in my day, but I would never cheat. I never had a relationship with a married person. That means everything to me. It's okay that you might love somebody's husband, but you have to know that there's a line you can't cross. You need to remember that somebody's out there for you. You can love somebody, but you can't act on every impulse.

Eventually, Will came back to me, but it was begrudgingly. He was still partying and not acting like an adult. One night, he was at the house with Danielle, and I went to my neighbor's house across the street. While I was there, Will came outside, and he was drunk, screaming in the street, yelling my name. There was snow on the ground. When I heard, I looked out the window. Then I'm yelling at him, "Where's the baby? Where's Danielle?" He's outside, drunk off his behind, and our daughter's only a couple of months old. He left her in the house by herself. I said, "Have you lost your mind?" I was so angry with him, but I still couldn't bring myself to actually throw him out.

27

That all changed when I got a call from my friend Peter, who also worked at the ASPCA. Peter had liked me before, but he was married, so nothing happened. He tried to talk to me again when Will and I broke up, but at this point, Peter and I were still just friends.

One day, he called and said, "Diane, I need to talk to you." I said, "What's up, Peter?" He said, "Will's going to leave you. I need you to know this." I was getting ready to buy this living room set for the apartment, and Peter says, "Honey, I think you need to hold on to your money." I asked, "What are you talking about?" He said, "Listen, Will told me he wants to get an apartment with me." I said, "Will? My Will?" He said, "Yeah." I said, "You're lying. You're just telling me this because you're mad at me for not going out with you." He said, "Diane, I swear, I'm not lying. Will's planning to leave you." To prove it, Peter let me listen in on a conversation between him and Will. I heard it for myself, Will talking about getting an apartment together. I said to myself, "Okay, so I'm going to one-up him," and I finally decided to throw Will out. When I told Will he had to leave, he kind of ignored me. But he started sleeping on the couch instead of in our bed.

I was mad he wouldn't leave, but I didn't know what to do. I knew that Peter liked me, so I told him, "Come on over. Let's talk." I guess I was afraid to be alone back then because I had been homeless and on my own for so long. Moving from house to house gets pretty old pretty fast. Who wants to live like that with a baby? I have this brand-new baby, four or five months old. So Peter came over that night and professed his love to me. I said, "Okay, whatever." Not exactly what he wanted to hear.

But then Peter started to grow on me. We went out a few times and sometimes talked all night. The problem was that Will was still living in my apartment. I was thinking, *This is ridiculous.* I have my own apartment, and I told Will I wanted him to go. But he said, "I'm not going anywhere." I said, "Oh, yeah, you are. You need to leave because this is my place, and I'm not going anywhere." He refused, so I said, "Okay, you're not going anywhere. That's fine. But it's over between you and me."

Even though I told Will it's over, it's done, I knew he didn't really believe me. So I decided to come into the house with Peter one night. When we walked in, Will said, "Hey, man, what's happening?" He hadn't figured out what was going on because Peter was his friend too. I said, "Well, Peter and I are dating, and you need to leave." He said, "I'm not going anywhere." I said, "Well, suit yourself," and I went into the bedroom with Peter and locked the door. I wouldn't do anything physical with Peter that night. We weren't doing anything in there. We were just watching TV, but I was thinking, *Damn, did Will leave yet? Is he going to leave, or is he going to try to break the door down?*

I knew Will was a lot of mouth, and anything could make him angry. He had wanted to leave me and live with Peter, but I'd flipped the script on him. I was pissed, thinking, *How dare you do that to me? I'm in survival mode. I've got a baby, and Peter's got a good job. Why am I going to be shit-out-of-luck and maybe have to move because Will doesn't know what he's going to do?*

Finally, I came out of the bedroom to go to the bathroom, and Will was still on the couch. I go back into the bedroom, and Peter's asking, "Do you want me to go talk to him?" I said, "No, I don't want you to say anything. This is not your business. This is between me and him. I asked Will to leave and told him the relationship was over weeks ago. He's been sleeping on the couch because he had nowhere to go." When I came out the second time, Will was gone, and I locked the front door.

Peter and I stayed together for about a year. He was a really nice guy. He had an ex-wife and two little girls. He was very attached to his daughters, but he was also very controlling and jealous. At some point, I couldn't deal with that. Overbearing is probably a better word to describe him. He was overbearing about anything I did. I couldn't breathe. I couldn't turn around without him asking, "What are you doing? Where are you going?"

And to be honest, I still had a soft spot for Will. When I started dating Peter, I was just really angry with Will. I was fuming. I was the mother lion protecting her cub.

One day, Will's dad, Daniel, came over and advocated Will's case. He asked me to give his son another chance. I said, "Hell, no, I'm not doing that." But then Danielle's first birthday rolled around, and my sister got a DJ for the party. That was a crazy thing to do, spending so much money on a first birthday, but when you're young, you do stupid things like that. My brother, David, even showed up for the party, even though we hadn't seen each other in months.

It was a really nice birthday party, and Will came, and he was playing with our daughter. Of course, I didn't have any dad in my life except my dad in England, and I always wanted my kids to have their father in their life. Will was very attentive to Danielle that day, and I found my feelings toward him softening. And Peter had become so overbearing.

Being with Peter just got to be unbearable for me, so I swapped men again. It was on my birthday, on March 13. I was twenty-two, and I didn't know who I wanted to spend my birthday with. I didn't know if I wanted to spend my birthday with Peter or Will. I was just swapping and moving back and forth mentally. I didn't know what I was doing. But eventually, I let Will back into my life, and he stayed in my life for almost ten years.

Danielle, Diane, and David

28

Neil was five, and Danielle was two. I was back living with Will. We never got married, but we were getting along okay. Still, my life felt empty in some ways. I started thinking a lot about my life back in England because I was the same age as my kids when I lived with the Harts. I wondered if it might be better for me to move back to England. There was no relationship between me and my mom at all, and Carolyn Hart was still my mom in my heart.

One day, I decided to call the number of my old house back in England. The Harts had "two-three-double-one" as a phone number. I had that number in my memory my entire life. One day, I called the telephone operator and asked her to dial that number, and a man answered the phone. I told him I was looking for Carolyn Hart, and he said, "I'm sorry, miss. We bought the house from her. She no longer lives here." But he said, "We have an address of where Mrs. Hart moved. Would you like us to give it to you?" And I said, "Oh, my God, yes."

I wrote a letter to that address, and Carolyn wrote me back. I asked about the other kids. "How's Tony? How's this one? How's that one?" She said, "Well, the only ones I've stayed in touch with are Luke and Eddie." She said Eddie came to visit her at least once a month.

Eddie was one of the kids I thought of as my brother when I lived with the Harts. Eddie was the goalie when we played soccer. Actually, we called it football in England. We had so much property that we actually had a goal, a real soccer goal. Eddie used to like people taking pictures of him. I think it made him feel like the big man of the house or whatever.

Carolyn gave Eddie my address in America, and that is how it started. We wrote back and forth, and I gave him my phone number. One day, Eddie called me up, and then we were talking all the time even though the calls were really expensive. Somehow, I became infatuated with Eddie through these phone calls. At that point, Will and I weren't doing well together. Eddie sent me a picture of himself, and he was really cute. I was thinking, *Wow! And there's nothing wrong with us getting together since we're not really brother and sister.* I thought, *Well, this might be the one. Let me go back and see what's going on.* I somehow got the money to fly to England. I went by myself. The foster mother taking care of Neil agreed to take care of Danielle while I was away.

When I arrived in London, Luke picked me up at the airport. He was my youngest brother in the house, and he was adopted by another family. He took me to see Carolyn Hart. She had moved from the really big house. Actually a movie producer owns that house now, and he renovated it. She had a lot of regret about selling that house. She sold it after her husband died, but she told me she wished she had never sold that house. When I went back there, the neighborhood was full of people that looked like they were lawyers and doctors, very successful people.

Guildford was once voted the prettiest village in England. Everything is rustic. You can't go into that village and change your house. No, it all has to stay the way it is. There are certain things you can do. On the inside of your house, you can do a lot of things, but on the outside, no. All the streets were cobblestoned and absolutely gorgeous.

Luke brought me to my mom's new house. She knew I was coming because Eddie told her. To be honest, I was most excited to see Eddie, who was more on my brain than my mom because his voice sounded sexy on the phone. He had a British accent, a gorgeous voice. He sent me this gorgeous picture, but it was a little, tiny picture. I didn't realize he was a little, tiny man. There was no way to know from the picture. He never mentioned that he was four-eleven, maybe five foot. He was my size, a very short, tiny fellow.

Both Williams were six foot. So when I saw Eddie, I'm thinking, *Jesus.* Almost right away, Eddie was saying, "Come on, Diane. Let's have a go. Let's have a go." But I was thinking, *Oh, no, I came all the way over here for this?* To put him off, I said, "I need to go see more of Mom."

When I got to her house, she got this spread out, teatime, they call it. I can remember it from when I lived there, but it all seemed so weird to me now because I had been in America for so long. They had the tea, macaroni, and buttered bread on the table, and I'm thinking, *Where are the burgers? Where's the fried chicken?* There were no big meats. That was it, just macaroni and cheese and bread. I'm realizing, *Oh, no. I've been Americanized. I've been spoiled.* They eat meat maybe twice a week. Meat is expensive, so they don't eat it like we do in America. I'm looking at the food, thinking, *Really? This is it?*

Later, I realized that my mom had put all her pictures of me in the attic. That really hurt. I guess she couldn't deal with it. At least, I want to believe she couldn't. When she had to go to the attic to find the pictures, I was thinking, *Wow, Mom, you didn't even keep one picture of me down here? You didn't have one picture of me in your Bible or nothing?* She didn't say anything about it, and I didn't say anything.

I wanted the pictures because that's all I had of me as a child. I told her I was grateful for everything she did for me, but I realized she had let me go emotionally. I know she wanted to adopt me back then, but it was different now. Maybe she felt she had no choice, but it really hurt that my pictures were out of sight. I really, really loved her. I never would have put pictures of her in my attic. They would always be close, near, and dear to me.

I wasn't sure how to process that whole experience.

Carolyn Hart took good care of me as a child. I did love her. I felt like she did right by me even if she didn't love me the way I loved her.

I don't know if she did really love me or didn't. All I know is that my pictures were in the attic. I know my dad, her husband, loved me. I know he did, and I don't doubt that she loved me. Maybe it was just too hard for her. Maybe she just had to put the pictures away because it was too hard.

I just chose to remember the fun, and I'll always be grateful to the Harts. They took me in and loved on me. They helped me get through a very important time. When I came to her, I was an infant, just a few months old. The Harts raised me up to nine years old. But when I went back to England, things were not the same. Yes, she did love me at one time, but I think she had to move on from the memories to get on with her life. She told me I could stay with her, but she wasn't the mom I remembered anymore.

I had my kids in America. I didn't want to take them away from their lives. If you don't come from money in England, there is not too much to do. I talked with my mom a little about the idea of moving back. She told me, "You can be a maid or a nanny." I said, "No. I can go back to America and do better than that." So I bade my farewells and left.

I loved her. I always loved her. If I didn't have the memories of that woman and family to lean on, my life in America would have been even harder. When I was being terribly abused, I knew it was wrong. It was not the way a family should be. I had been part of a loving, healthy family in England. I knew what positive experiences were like.

I wasn't a victim like people who grow up in violence and abuse from day one, who grow up never knowing what it's like to be loved. I had a loving family. I just couldn't swim the ocean to get back to them. I had to come to terms with the fact that that part of my life was over. But I had sworn I would go back to see her one day, and I did.

When I was leaving, my mom warned me that Eddie was sweet on me. "You have to be careful, Diane." She was very motherly to me. "You have two children in America. You have to think about them," and she told me Eddie had a lot of issues. I understood. I was ready to leave him behind, but Eddie wanted to come to America.

For some reason, I felt duty bound to have sex with Eddie before I left. That was stupid. It was crazy because I couldn't even feel him in me. He was that little, seriously. I'm not saying that to be rude, but he was just little, period, all the way around. He didn't know how to make love or anything. So now I'm thinking, *Oh, Lord. What have I done?*

I ended up bringing him back to America. I knew he wanted to leave England, but I didn't realize he was really in love with me. I wasn't in love with him. I was in love with the idea of the past and attracted to him as a kid. But now, it was all a big mistake.

I was still living with Will at the time, so I had to tell everyone that Eddie was my brother. He returned to New York, and stayed for a few months. Will said, "Y'all are doing something. I know y'all are doing it." I said, "Eddie is my brother. Stop it." I never copped to it, but yeah, when Will left the apartment, I fooled around with Eddie. The whole time, I was thinking, *What in the heck am I doing?*

I tried to help Eddie, but all he wanted to do was fool around. I was saying, "You got to go back. We won't be able to keep this secret. You're going to end up telling Will that you're messing with me, and he's going to kill you." Because of his height, Eddie was always trying to prove himself, saying, "I'm the best football player. I'm the best this. I'm the best that." It really got on my nerves, so I told him, "You've got to go home, back to England. It was fun at first, but now it's not." It was a crazy time, and I told him he had to go back. I made him go back.

I never spoke to him after that. I let it go. He sent me letters and begged me to stay in touch, but I let it go. It was a mistake. Unfortunately, because of my sexual abuse and everything, I sometimes had sex for the wrong reasons. It wasn't working. Eddie wasn't making me feel whole. It wasn't making me feel anything. It just did not.

Eddie, Carolyn Hart, and Diane during her visit back to England

29

For a long time, I let Neil live with his foster mother, Anna. I'm not going to lie. I liked my freedom. It was easier having him stay with her temporarily so I could have just one child to focus on. I said to Anna, "You know what? You're like a grandmother to him, so we'll share him." I honestly thought he was better off with her at times.

She offered to pay for Neil to go to Catholic school. You've got to remember, I lived in the ghetto. Anna and her husband lived in the suburbs. I didn't want my son to live in the ghetto just because I had to. My house didn't look like it, but I lived in the ghetto. I had a nice little apartment next to an abandoned building, but the inside was nice.

I wanted Neil to have the opportunity to go to a better school. Anna was paying for it and everything. At the time, I didn't realize that Anna's husband was cheating on her, and she had totally immersed herself in my son's life. She had become too emotionally attached to him. Neil's principal told me Anna slapped a teacher because the teacher failed my son in first grade. They failed him because they found out Anna was doing all his work.

The other problem was that Neil was also gaining a huge amount of weight. He weighed 151 pounds. The principal of his school told me, "Miss Diane, you have to get your son back and have him live with you. Look how big he is. He's going to have a heart attack and die if this continues. He's only seven years old." They were ready to call DSS if I didn't take him, so I said, "Okay. Let him finish the school year, and I'll take him in the summertime."

Anna heard about this, and she didn't like it. So she called the police and started making up lies about me, and the police came to my house. Will and I were still living together, and the police told me that my son said that Will and I were having sex in front of him when he stayed with us. I couldn't believe what I was hearing. I told the police, "Let me tell you something. I'm not going to deny having sex in my apartment. But if I have sex and my son is staying with us, my son is on the sofa bed in the living room, watching TV. My bedroom door is locked. When I open my door, I have my pajamas on, and my boyfriend has his sweatpants on. My son has never seen anything inappropriate."

I had to go down to the DSS the next day to deal with this mess, and I was surprised to see Bryan there. Bryan was the social worker who had signed all my checks when I was a minor. Back then, I was too young to sign for any of my own checks, so Bryan took care of all my financial stuff. He paid my rent, my light bill. He gave me food stamps to get food, made sure I had my Medicaid, made sure I was doing the right thing. He just helped me with other resources too. I had kept in touch with Bryan over the years, and now I find out he's the head of sex investigations for DSS.

It turned into a hot mess that day at the DSS office. Anna showed up with her adult son. Neil and Will came with me. Things got tense, and Will started fighting with Anna's son in the lobby. Will was shouting, "You motherfucker." He couldn't beat up Anna, so he went after her son. The poor security guards were trying to deal with the whole situation. In the meantime, Bryan pulled me upstairs. Bryan said, "Diane, sit in this room. I'm going to talk to Neil."

After an hour, Bryan called me into his office, dealing with me directly. He said, "Diane, take your son and go home. Never, ever, ever let that woman near him again." I said, "Bryan, what the hell. Why did she do that?" I was crying, and he said, "That woman's crazy,

Diane." He talked to Neil, and Neil said that Anna told him to say that stuff about me having sex in front of him. He didn't know what he was saying. He had no clue at all.

So, after we take Neil home, Anna called me, crying. "Please, please. Let me see Neil." And I said, "Leave me alone." I was sitting in my window on the fire escape. I was thinking, *God, this woman is never going to leave me alone. I'm never going to be free of her. I wish to God that she could be out of my life forever.* Well, two months later, I get a call telling me that Anna's in the hospital, and she's very, very sick. She wants to see Neil, but I'm not buying this story. I call the hospital, and I ask what's going on. They said, "If you're asking if she's going to die tomorrow, the answer is no." I said, "Okay, then she's fine."

She died two days later, but I honestly had no clue she was dying. I really thought it was her exaggerating, falling down on the ground, yelling, "Aye, Papi," with her antics again. I had no idea. I was devastated. I called Bryan, and I was crying. I said, "Bryan, she died, and I feel like it's my fault." I told him about when I was on the fire escape, and I was talking to God and complaining that Anna would never leave me alone. Bryan said, "Diane, do you think you're God? Do you think you have the power to kill this woman? Do you?" He said, "Girl, get it together."

Bryan set me real straight, real quick. He said, "Diane, do you think you're fucking God? Do you think you can sit in your room and say, 'She is not going to leave me alone,' and God's just going to come and take her? Just stop it right now and go on with your life because you had no control over that. She knew what she was doing with Neil that whole time. She was a foster parent, and she knew that Neil was your biological child. She understood that she would have to give him back to you. She should have never made you feel guilty and all that kind of stuff."

Bryan said, "You had nothing to do with her death, sweetie." But, my God, I felt so guilty because I knew I hurt her by taking Neil away from her. I was so angry because she hurt me. She tried to get Neil back by lying about me, and that was devious. What she did could've gotten me locked up. Bryan really had to snap me out of it, though. He had to say it was crazy. It was crazy. He is another one of those angels in my life.

Years later, when I found out that Bryan died, that hurt. I went to see him one day at his office, and they told me he had a massive heart attack. I never got to show him that I graduated from college. I had gone down there to show him my diplomas, and they told me he had passed. That was really sad. That was another loss for me because Bryan was like a surrogate father to me. He would pull me out of all my messes. He said, "Girl, you don't know it, but you're a true survivor." He said, "Diane, it's in you. You've just got to find it. You've just got to keep fighting."

30

I didn't see much of my mom over the years. One day, I heard that Mack ended up leaving her. Then, all of a sudden, I hear from her. She wanted me back in her life. She wanted her daughter. She also wanted to reconnect with my brother, David. It sounds crazy, but I was open to it. I later learned that abused kids want to be loved by their parents. No matter what they've gone through, they still want to be loved by their parents, so I went to see her. She was crying, and she was a mess. Mack had left her for somebody half her age. At that point, David and I both helped to support her, and we were willing to do it for her. But some things about people just don't change.

One time, I went to visit my mom, and she was screaming and yelling at Mary. Mary ran in the bathroom, and my mother put holes in the bathroom door, trying to get at her. My sister was yelling, "You're crazy. You're crazy!"

My sister would talk back to my mother. I never had the nerve to talk back to her, but that all changed the day she tried to swing at Neil. We were visiting her, and she threw something, and it almost hit him in the head. It was some metal, brass thing she had on the table, and my mother was just going crazy. She wasn't trying to actually hit Neil with it, don't get me wrong, but when she threw that thing, it almost hit my son.

I grabbed her arm for the first time in my life. It wasn't easy because my mother's five-seven and I'm five-feet. I told her, "You will never, ever, ever touch my kids. Ever." I meant it, and I brought her to her knees almost just with my hand. I wasn't trying to hurt her, but I forced her into a chair. I shouted, "Now sit down. Sit down." And I was serious. She yelled, "Get the fuck out of my house!" Oh, you should have heard her. "Oh, yeah," I said. "I'm leaving because you are crazy. I'm getting the hell out." I took my son, and she never, ever hit my kids again. Ever.

31

When I first got with Will, he would have a few drinks, but he wasn't an alcoholic. As the years passed by, he became a drug addict and alcoholic. I was the enabler. I definitely was enabling him because you could not tell that an alcoholic lived in my house by the way it looked. I kept it clean.

We were living on Loring Place and West 183rd Street in the Bronx, down the road from Bronx Community College. It was a nice little side street. In the Bronx, you can have three or four very nice roads, and then you can end up with four or five deserted blocks. Our apartment happened to be very near the college, and it was also across the street from a military station. It was never going to get too shabby because there was too much around there that was good. They ended up building the elementary school PS-15 right next to my building, so my kids were in good shape as far as that went.

But my self-esteem was in the toilet. I'd wear new clothes and ask Will, "How does this look on me?" And he'd say, "Oh, whatever, you look fine." So I stopped caring about what I looked like because he never said anything positive. He didn't hit me or anything like that, but it was more subtle. It was also verbal abuse. He'd say, "You're nothing. You're shit. You're never going to be anything. You're always going to be on welfare. You're never going to have anything." You keep hearing it, and it wears you down. My house was beautiful, but I didn't buy anything for me. I didn't value myself.

Eventually, I became just his caregiver. I was caring for my kids and him. Despite all that, I wanted another child, but I didn't want to have three kids by three different baby-daddies. I'll be honest. I already knew I wouldn't stay with Will much longer, but I wanted another child. So I got pregnant by him, and my son, Michael, was born.

When I was in the hospital after I gave birth, I told Will, "You need to clean up the house before I bring the baby back." Well, his idea of cleaning was to start by pulling everything out of the cupboards. It was like military cleaning. And then he decided not only would he clean, but he would also start painting the apartment.

I had to take a taxi back from the hospital because he was too drunk to pick me up. I came home to random chaos. There was nowhere to put the baby down. Every room was destroyed, pulled apart. I had to take Michael and put him in Neil's arms. I said, "Do not put him down. Just sit here and hold him until I get my bedroom cleaned up." Will was drunk off his ass.

I'm thinking, *How did I get myself into this mess?* I was pretty upset because William, the first William, was the love of my life, and he turned into a drug addict and alcoholic. And now it happened all over again. I was thinking, *How did I pick the same type of guy?* I had no clue what I was doing. I was in a pickle. I had three kids. I'm wondering, *How am I going to make it with three kids?*

I knew my relationship with Will was over. I think women often know relationships aren't working, but they don't want to take action to do something about it. They know they're not going to stay for the long haul, but they're trying to figure out how they're going to make it on their own. I think a lot of women leave men emotionally way before we leave them physically. We just can't get out.

I had two breaking points with Will.

One involved my friend Jackie. We met when we lived in a group home together. Jackie's parents were dead. Some kids are stronger than others, and Jackie just couldn't deal with it anymore after her parents died. She started drinking and getting high and doing drugs.

She ended up getting AIDS.

One day, Jackie called me and told me we needed to talk. I said, "Okay," so she came over and sat down. She said, "Diane, Will came by to cop some crack from me." I said, "Crack?" She said, "Yeah, Diane, I'm not talking about blow. I'm talking about crack. And then he wanted to fuck me." I said, "He wanted to fuck you?" And she said, "Yeah, but I said, 'No.' I didn't fuck him because of you and because I'm HIV positive. You know that." Jackie said, "I'm coming to tell you because you got kids, and you need to know what he's up to. I'm doing this because we've been friends for years."

She said, "I need to let you know that this is what he's doing behind your back. He wanted to have sex with me, and he wanted me to get high with him." I believed her. I one-hundred-percent believed her. I thought, *Oh my God. I've got to get out of this relationship for real.* So I confronted Will, but he denied it all. I knew it was true, so I refused to let him touch me, not even with a condom after I found out about that.

A few nights later, I wake up because it sounded like it was raining out the living room. I was in bed, hearing a sound like a bottle of water pouring on the rug, thinking, *What in the world?* I go into the living room and turn on the light, and there's Will peeing on my Christmas tree and the gifts underneath. He thought he was outdoors and the tree was a bush. That's how drunk he was. I saw him shaking it off, putting it back in his pants.

When I tell my friends this story, they laugh about it. I can laugh at it now, but it wasn't funny then. Even though we weren't legally married, he was supposed to be my husband. We had been together almost ten years, and there he is, urinating on my tree, on my Christmas, on my dreams for my kids. He's urinating on Fisher Price toys, learning toys for my son. My mind is saying to me, *You chose this*, and then *Uh-uh, no, I did not choose this.* Then something said, *Well, why do you keep choosing the same messed up people?* It was a back-and-forth thing.

That night broke the camel's back.

32

The next day, I ended up at this Presbyterian church at the end of my road. I'd never been in there before. I have no idea why I went, but I just felt compelled. I was in the back, and tears were just running down my face. I couldn't hear the sermon. I couldn't hear anything. I had these two-dollar sneakers on that day. I'll never forget it, these two-dollar penny-ante sneakers. God, how am I going to do this? How am I going to do this?

Then something stirred inside me. It wasn't audible. I didn't hear it out loud, but I heard it in my spirit: *You're gonna do it one day at a time, one foot in front of the other. You're gonna take it one day at a time, but you do have to leave Will.* That's the revelation I got in the back of the church. I didn't even know what was going on. I didn't even know what the sermon was. But now I knew what I had to do. As I look back now, I truly believe that I know where that voice in my head was coming from. It had to be God.

Before the church service finished, I went home, and I told Will to leave. I made it clear I wasn't kidding, and he said, "I hope you fall on your fucking face." I responded, "Well, you know what, Will? I wish you the best of luck too." He was trying to hurt me, but I just wished him luck. Then, he shouted, "Where the hell am I supposed to go? I have nowhere to go. You're going to just throw me out?"

So I said, "Okay, I'm going to bring Danielle into my room, and you can live in her room." Even though the relationship was over, it's hard to divorce emotionally. You don't just stop caring, and I still saw some good in him. He had positive qualities, but he had an alcoholic father and a mother who was passive.

I couldn't just kick Will out because he was the kids' father. He had also renovated our whole apartment. I'll give him that. He was very handy. He was a carpenter and a good electrician and everything.

Eventually, Will moved out and ended up at a place on Davidson Avenue, but it was a mess over there. Around his house, the dealers would run to your car to sell you drugs. It was a horrible neighborhood, the worst place for him to be. One time, I let my kids go over there with him because Will's sister was supposed to be there too. I figured if she was there, the kids would be fine. Well, something in my spirit told me to go check on things. When I got there, the couch was half open. My baby Michael was about two years old at the time, and he was kind of sleeping on the couch. My daughter was eating some kind of cold cereal, and Will was in the bedroom with a prostitute, smoking crack. Luckily, my daughter didn't have a clue what he was doing.

I snatched up my kids and got them out of there. I told him, "I'm not going to tell your parents. I'm not going to say anything, but you need help. When you decide that you need help and want help, call me and let me know. But until then, you have to come to my house to see the kids. That has to be the way it is."

But he didn't come by to see our kids because he was so strung out, drugged out, big-time. Once I was no longer in his life, the material part of his life just fell completely apart. Nothing was being washed. Everything was filthy around the house. It was what crack houses look like. When he moved in, it was a brand-new apartment building that they had just rehabbed, but Will totally trashed it.

I called his mother and told her what was going on. Will's sister Allie was a police officer, and I called her also. I said, "You need to come to my house. Will is in trouble." I told her about the condition of where he was living. I said, "You need to go over there and check on him." Allie did. Later, she called me back and said, "You're right. It's a fucking mess, and he's not listening to us." I said, "Well there's nothing you can do. We can't really do anything until he wants help. You got to know that my kids are not going over there anymore." And she said, "I totally understand."

At this time in New York City, there was a crazy person that was throwing lighter fluid into subway booths and setting them on fire. The people who worked in the booths were killed because they couldn't get out in time. Well, some whore Will was living with called the police and told them Will was setting the fires. Who knows why she said that, but one day, I drove to his house to get something from him, and the police were there. They pulled him into the squad car, and I asked, "What in the hell is going on?" They told me he was being arrested for murder. I'm not kidding you. I can't make this stuff up.

I called his sister Allie because she's a police officer, and she said, "I'll get down there." She found out exactly what was going on. Will ended up in jail for a couple of days until they straightened it out and realized what that whore said was nonsense. But they found drug paraphernalia in his house, and he got in trouble for that, which forced him into rehab.

Despite everything, I never forgot he was my kids' father. It was important for them to have a relationship with him, but not in that condition. I got in touch with a friend who knew somebody at Daytop Village, a rehab center in upstate New York. They agreed to get him in there.

33

After I broke up with Will, I thought, God, I don't know what to do. I got three kids, and I'm all by myself. Danielle was in kindergarten, Neil was in fifth grade, and Michael was a baby. I did what I could to make ends meet.

I remember going downstairs in my building one day, and there was this lady living there. She was an Indian lady, and she was making good money. She didn't like to clean her house. She asked me to clean her house, and she would pay me. And I did. I went down there every weekend and cleaned her house. After, I'd go to the nearby supermarket, Bravo's, and they'd have some kind of meat on sale. Let's say they had chicken, whole chickens on sale for $2.50 each. I'd buy ten of them. That would last for a while. I did what I needed to make the money stretch as far as possible.

Then I met this lady across the hall from me. She had a bunch of kids, and her kids started playing with my kids. One day, I'm asking about her big family, and she tells me, "Girl, these ain't my actual kids. These is foster kids." I said, "Okay," but I was still not getting it. She goes, "Well, the government pays me money to let them live with me." I said, "They pay you money?" *Ding ding ding!* There's a bell going off in my head. I said, "What do you mean, they pay you?" And she explained it all to me.

I thought, *I gotta be home with my kids. What's a couple more?* I filled out the foster parent application. I found out they didn't care if you were on public assistance. I guess they figured, "We're giving you some kind of assistance, so at least you could do something to help us out."

First, they gave me Juan. He came when he was eighteen months. After a year, they told me they were going to move Juan to another foster home because he had a brother named Charles, and they didn't think I could handle the two of them. I said, "How old's the brother?" They said, "Five months." I told them, "I'm home anyway, so it doesn't matter. You can let him stay for a couple of months, and let's see how it works."

It all worked out okay, so DSS got excited, and the next year, they wanted to give me another one. I figured, why not? His name was Monty. By that time, I had two four-year-olds and two five-year-olds. It was like having quads. I used to dress them alike so I could figure out who was who in the park. And don't forget, I still had my two older kids, Neil and Danielle, so we had a full house.

Having the foster kids helped me out because I really didn't want to put my own kids in day care. I said, "I can go to college, I can raise my kids, and I can have foster kids." When them checks started coming, things got a lot easier.

One day, the DSS folks asked me if I wanted to adopt the kids instead of just fostering them. I told them, "Look, I already have three children, and I'm on welfare. How are you asking me to adopt these kids?" They said, "Well, this is what we'll do for you if you adopt them. We'll give you a thousand dollars a kid per month." I said, "What? Okay, wait a minute." That is way more than they were giving for foster care. And they said, "We'll also give you Medicaid for the kids until they're twenty-one," because I was worried what would happen if they got sick. I do the math in my head, thinking, *Okay, even with my college two-year degree, I'm not going to make this kind of money. This way, I can still stay home with my kids and raise them all.*

They call these kids "hardship adoptions." If it's a hardship adoption, they pay more because it's very hard to get people to adopt siblings—very, very hard. If the kid has ADHD, which all three of them had, the rates go up more. When I first adopted the boys, I had no idea they had ADHD. Those diagnoses came out later. I was thinking, *Okay, nobody told me this. Nobody told me that.*

The first foster care check was about $900. Now you've got to remember, I'm used to seeing a welfare check for $150 every two weeks. I was thinking, *What the . . . ?* When that check came in, we had a good time, and I was buying them anything they wanted. They had a clothing allowance, but I still bought stuff for everybody.

Then I got another one for $1,600. Then I got another one. That was $900 again. I was thinking, *Jeez, this is pretty cool. I'm making more money staying home than I could make working some lousy job.* I didn't have the level of education to make that kind of money, and I didn't have to pay any babysitters.

I had so much food that I used to give it out to other people in my building. I would get the food from WIC, which is women, infants, and children food assistance. I had four kids on WIC at the same time. I had so much milk, there were people knocking on my door. "Diane, can I have a gallon of milk?" I would give it to them. We also had the cheese, the big blocks of cheese.

The kids were doing good living with me. If you look at the big picture, it seems like a lot of money. But if you break the payments down, it comes out to $0.23 an hour or something like that. You're talking about being somebody's twenty-four-hour care. You're not going to do it just for the money because you are basically giving up your life. I was at home with those kids all day. I was always going to meetings with social workers. I had to go and arrange their IEPs, which are individualized education programs. When I really needed a break, I could take them to respite care.

I treated them kids good. I did. They had fun Christmases, thousand-dollar Christmases. Every Christmas, I had no problem spending lots of money on them. They had two computers in the living room when computers first came out. I mean, they had every name-brand system thing, everything. As I look back on those days, the only thing I regret was them not knowing God, not taking them to church.

I know people will say, "Oh, you just do it for the money." Well, some people do, yeah. You hear the horror stories. But remember that there are also horror stories about kinship foster care. That's where these people have siblings who are drug addicts, so they agree to step in to provide foster care for their siblings' kids. But then they end up enabling their sibling to stay drug-addicted so they can keep getting the checks to care for the kids. I mean, it's a huge scam in the cities. The thing is, if you want to pay for twenty-four-hour care, institutionalization, it's going to cost $100,000 a kid. I'm just keeping it real, keeping it honest.

What I get from people sometimes is, "Oh, you got so many kids. How much money are you getting?" Why are you worrying about what I get? You could go out there and do the same thing I'm doing. But other people are not lining up. I don't see anybody lining up to do this work. Do you think it's okay for a kid to stay in an institution and have nobody ever touch them or show them any affection? They can end up like some animal behind bars.

And you're wondering why we got all these people in jail. Most of the people in jail have been in foster care, or they didn't have parents or were abused. That's a huge population of people. Am I thinking about adopting more kids someday? Yeah, maybe two more kids.

34

When I broke up with Will, I was by myself for about eighteen months. Then, one day, the first William called me out of the blue. That was a shock. It had been five years since I last heard from him. I heard he got married in South Carolina and had three kids with his new wife. But that day, he was calling me from a jail.

He says, "Hi," and I'm asking, "Who is this?" And he says, "William" And I said, "Boy, I know you're not calling me. Your son is almost nine years old. I have not heard from you since he was four." I said, "I don't even want to talk to you."

He said, "Diane, I have an explanation. First of all, I couldn't get in touch with you because your number wasn't listed, so please just hear me out." And I said, "Okay, all right. I'll hear you out." He was right about that. My number was unlisted for a long time, but somehow, it had gotten listed recently, so that's how he tracked me down.

He explained how he ended up in jail. He told me he had planned to divorce his wife because he found out she was cheating on him with a plumber. William wanted the divorce, but his wife didn't. So, she decided to claim that he sexually molested her daughter. Not one of their biological children but one of hers from an earlier relationship.

DSS told William that if he admitted he did abuse his stepdaughter, then he would go to therapy for six months and the charges would go away. But he said, "I would rather go to hell than admit I did something like that. I didn't do it. She's only saying this because we're getting ready to divorce." She wanted custody of all the kids, but he wanted some custody of his three biological kids. Since he didn't take the plea deal, he ended up going to jail.

When William told me that his wife had done this to him, I believed him. I just knew that what his wife said was a lie. You know people, and I knew those accusations were not true. William's not somebody I met while he was serving time in jail. I really knew him. When we were going together, you should have seen the women going after him, even when he was a drug addict. It was ridiculous. He was very much a ladies' man, very much. Girls wanted to fight me because they wanted to be with him. I told William, "I'm not fighting anybody for you." He was saying, "I don't even want those girls!" But they wanted to fight me because I was Caucasian-skinned, and they were saying to him, "Why don't you stay with your own kind?" But William would say, "You can't tell me who to love. Diane's who I love." I knew him as a person, and I knew he would never abuse a little girl.

And this woman he married in South Carolina, she was absolutely gorgeous. She made me look like a vagabond. Seriously, she was a tall model-type, an African American girl, absolutely gorgeous.

I'm shocked about everything he's telling me, and I'm just trying to take it all in. Even though he's telling me he's getting divorced, I said, "I don't deal with married people." I said, "Regardless of whatever you're going through with her, you guys are still married, and you're in jail." He tells me he's been in jail for four years. "So they convicted you?" I said. "Yeah, because she testified against me," he said. I don't know what to think at this point. As his friend, I don't believe he's guilty because I just know him, but I'm not sure what to think.

He actually sent me the whole testimony and transcripts from the trial and everything. There was no evidence of any penetration. There was nothing in her panties, but they didn't have DNA back then. There was none of that. William found out later that the prosecutors twisted his wife's arm to testify. The lawyers told her, "We know that you have been getting welfare illegally. Your husband has been working all along, so we are going to charge you with welfare fraud if you don't say he did this to your daughter." They scared her into testifying against him, but now her nonsense has caused this whole mess. Anyway, I thought it over, and I believed him. I said, "William, I believe you."

Then, I went down to South Carolina to see him at the prison. At first, they wouldn't allow me to see him because he was still married to her. The way I got to see him was because Neil was his son, and William's name was on his birth certificate. I had the right to let Neil see his father, so I got to see William.

He was a changed man. He wasn't Slick Rick anymore. He had a lot of weight on him, but he was muscular too. He loved God, and he was very, very spiritual. He talked about God on the phone every day, like he was ministering to me. I found my feelings for him changing. I don't know if I started to fall back in love with him or fell in love with the God in him. To be honest, I think I probably fell in love with both.

It wasn't until William went to jail that he got saved. I think being accused of something you didn't do was very sobering. William was very strong, a big guy, and he had a very charismatic personality. While he was in jail, he became head of the Christian ministry. He stayed with the whole Christian community, and when he came out, that's how he stayed. He never looked back, and he never took another drink. He never smoked crack, and he never sniffed coke again. He just didn't. He walked away from everything.

When I went to see him, this one prison guard pulled me aside. She said, "Miss, I've known a lot of prisoners, but this is the first one I've ever known who I really think is innocent." That really hit home with me. I was thinking, *Wow. God, are you trying to tell me something?* I didn't ask that woman to come and tell me anything. Anyway, after I visited William, he went up for parole, but he was denied. He ended up getting out for good behavior one year later, so at least he didn't have to do his full ten-year sentence.

He wanted to come up to New York to see me, but I wouldn't let him until he showed me his legal divorce papers. I told him that he could not come until he proved the marriage was over. I'm not one for breaking up marriages. I did not want to be the reason he and his wife were breaking up, and I was clear about that. I also needed a couple of years between him and the other Will.

After he got out of prison, his wife wanted him back with her. When I heard that, I thought, *That doesn't make sense. How do you want him back if he did something so horrible to your child?* I would want him hung on the cross and burned if I thought he hurt my child. So that's another reason I knew the sex abuse charges weren't true.

Finally, I told William he could come up to New York, and we got back together after being apart for ten years. Since I was a foster parent, we couldn't live together because of the sex abuse conviction. He ended up having to get a separate apartment, and he lived there with Neil. But we were together otherwise in every sense of the word.

William and Diane

35

My brother, David, and I stayed in touch on and off over the years, but our relationship was strained. He was into drugs for a while, and when he was, he would steal from me. He would try to pretend things in my apartment were just lost, but I knew better. I was thinking, You stole my necklace, and now you're pretending to help me look for it. This is ridiculous.

At Christmas, I liked having lots of things under the tree. I didn't have a lot of money, so sometimes I would take gold wrapping paper and wrap empty boxes to make my tree look nice. One day, my brother ripped open those boxes, looking for stuff to steal. It was just pathetic. I realized I couldn't help him because he was out doing things I couldn't deal with. Finally, I said, "I'm not helping you anymore." I had to draw a line.

One year later, David went to my mother's house, but he was very sick. He had been living on the streets and was looking really bad. My mother opened the door, and she took one look at him and decided to help. She worked at a hospital, so she took him there. He was diagnosed with pneumonia and AIDS. That news changed my mother's whole concept of him. All of a sudden, she loved her son. She realized he was going to die, and she wanted to make it right. She ended up switching to work on the AIDS ward to help care for him, and she did a lot of overtime work when my brother was in there.

After my brother got better and left the hospital, he went to live with my mother. At that point, she was living in a place called the Mark Terrace Apartments in the Bronx. The manager of the building had a daughter named Rosie. She was a drug addict who also had AIDS. David and Rosie ended up getting together. My brother was very good-looking, an Italian-looking type of fellow. After a couple of months, he and Rosie ended up getting married.

Rosie already had AIDS, so David said, "We can get married because I'm not going to hurt her. She's got it, and I've got it." But then, both of them decide they wanted to be parents—drug addict parents. I'm thinking, *Really?* And my mother said, "David, do not do that." But David allowed it to happen, and Rosie got pregnant. David always wanted a kid. He figured he'd straighten out his life and take care of his new baby. But my brother didn't live to see his daughter born.

Rosie was angry that my mom didn't support them getting married. The next time David got really sick, Rosie took my brother away from my mother, even though she had worked long double and triple shifts to care for him. Rosie was his legal wife, so my mother had no choice.

In the end, Rosie took my brother to Long Island Hospital, and my mother couldn't do anything about it. One day, William and I decided to go see David, but there was a really bad snowstorm, and the highways were shut down. We took the commuter train, and we walked in the snow a mile and a half to get there.

David was unconscious when we got there, and he looked like somebody from the Auschwitz concentration camp. He was unconscious, and William started praying over him and speaking this prayer of salvation. My brother never answered or said anything, but I did see one tear come down the side of his eye. I want to believe that my brother accepted Jesus as his Lord and Savior that night. He died later that week.

I know my mother felt bad about what happened to David when he was a kid. She knows that David was out on the streets because of what she and Mack did, even if she didn't admit it. But she tried everything in her power to be there for him at the end. I have to give her credit for that. Rosie was the one who took my brother away.

David told Rosie, "I don't want my mother to be there when I die." Rosie told me he said that. I never told my mother that, and I'm never going to do that to her. I was angry at my mother too, but I wasn't angry to the point where I felt that she shouldn't be able to say goodbye to her child. I really saw her make a gallant effort to be there for him.

My mother didn't get to go to David's funeral. She didn't get his ashes. She didn't get anything. Rosie threw his ashes into the Hudson River in New York. My mother never got to see him, say goodbye, nothing. Talk about "reap what you sow." At that point, my mother reaped what she sowed.

After losing my brother, I think she started to really value me. I think she needed some solace, somebody strong to be there for her, and I tried to be there for her as much as I could. But I was also angry because I blamed her, indirectly, for what happened to David. I know she never would have put a gun to his head, but the end result of her actions was still the same. He was dead.

After he died, Rosie gave birth. David has a daughter that my mother and I have never seen. The reason we haven't seen my niece is because Rosie never forgave my mother for trying to talk her and David out of having a baby.

Rosie's still alive, and she kind of wants a relationship with me now, but I'm just at this point where I can only deal with one thing at a time. I'm going to continue to pray for my niece. She's now nineteen and doing good, but we haven't had any contact. Rosie's sister is the one who actually raised her because Rosie was a drug addict. They also have issues with biracial families, so that complicates things between me and her. I just let it go. I figure my niece will find us if it's meant to be. She looks exactly like my brother. I pray for her, and I just leave it like that. I can't be the martyr for everybody. I can't.

36

David died of AIDS in 1993, and the disease was a terrifying thing for me. His death really brought AIDS up front and personal because he was my brother. I felt like I had to worry if everybody had AIDS. Since I couldn't figure out who had it and who didn't, I wasn't taking any chances. To be on the safe side, I generalized that all men had it, so William and I always used condoms.

After William had been living in New York for a while, we decided we were going to try to have another child. Before we started to have sex without a condom, I needed to make sure that AIDS was not an issue. Well, come to find out that it was an issue. I got tested, and I was negative. He got tested, and he told me he was positive. He broke down crying and said, "I don't think you're going to stay with me, and I don't blame you if you don't," that kind of stuff. When I first found out he was HIV-positive, I was throwing up, had diarrhea, and just felt awful. I thought, *Did he rub himself on me? Did a drop get on me?* Even though we used condoms, there's always a chance. Eventually, I had a second test, which came back negative, so that brought me relief.

Even so, there was definitely a lot of anxiety and fear. It changed things for a while. I told him I wasn't going to have sex with him. I told him he could still stay with me, but we weren't going to have sex. We didn't have sex for seven months, but I'm a woman. I missed the sex with him. So he found a way to make me happy without taking any chances. Let's just put it like that, and I did whatever I could to make him happy with my hands or whatever.

Then I said, "This is crazy." After a while, I had to come to terms with the fact that he was HIV-positive, so we went to a doctor. He told us about the strongest condoms and Nonoxynol 9, which is a contraceptive foam. We were very, very safe. We hardly did any French-kissing because gums sometimes bleed. When you know that somebody has AIDS, it's different. He was always very loving toward me. I mean, we made up for the intimacy in other ways, with back rubs, massages, all kinds of stuff.

I have to give William credit. He was very careful, and he took total responsibility. I never had to say, "Do you have a condom on?" He never, ever let me be fearful like that. I mean, he knew how dangerous it was.

And this is where God gave us a favor because we really wanted to have another baby together. We got our baby, just not the way we expected. I got a call from DSS, and we ended up getting a foster child when she was just twenty-one days old. Her name is Carrie, and we just fell in love with her right from the start. We started the adoption process after she had been with us just a month. William never actually adopted her or any of the kids. He couldn't because of the sex abuse conviction. No judge was going to let that happen, but I legally adopted Carrie, and once she was legally mine, then she was ours.

At this point, we were thinking about moving out of New York, but then DSS told me they had another baby for me. I told them, "No, I don't have any room. What are you talking about?" They said, "Well, her name is Cora, and she's Carrie's sister." I'm thinking, *If I go forward, this adoption is going to keep me in New York another two-plus years.*

William and I talked about it, and he said, "Diane, we just can't leave her. That's Carrie's sister." So we got Cora when she was three days old, a gorgeous, little, dark-skinned baby. I said, "Oh my God, William, she looks just like you." You would think Cora was his biological kid. He had that baby on his chest every day. As they got older, Cora and Carrie would fight to sit next to William. I had to sit on the other side. I couldn't even get next to William, but I thought it was adorable. I always wanted my kids to grow up with their father. Carrie and Cora were my kids, and in my heart, he was their father.

You would never believe they're not his children. God gave us what we wanted. We just didn't make those children. We were blessed. We never had a real financial problem. We had two apartments, and we did everything with the kids.

I had a very strong respect for William. I really respected him as a person. I think it was more than love. With some people, love is more a lust thing, but we had a mutual respect. We were best friends. We enjoyed each week. We started and finished each other's sentences. We enjoyed being together and spent a lot of time together.

We were so blessed that I would even still help out my ex, the other William. I had never asked him for child support for either of our two kids. Why should I go after him? He didn't have anything, and God was blessing me. Sometimes I even gave Will money on the down-low because he'd want to take Danielle and Michael out, but he didn't have any money. I'd say, "Here, take fifty dollars. Take them to the movies." I knew it was important for them to spend time with him.

He would say, "Diane, I want to see the kids, but I don't have any money." I'd tell him, "Well, just come on by, and I'll throw some money out the window when you get here." I would throw the envelope out of the window to him. Then he'd ring the bell, take them, and bring them back. The kids would come back with smiles on their faces, and that was what was important to me. I didn't know my own dad, so I was hell-bent on my kids knowing their father.

37

It was not easy trying to raise so many kids at once, especially the boys. Juan was the most rebellious, and unfortunately, the other two boys followed behind him. I think they felt like the Three Musketeers when they realized they could get away with crap. They realized the consequences we gave them were limited. The boys said, "They're not going to hit us; they're not going to do that to us." William would tell them, "Listen, you're going to act right, or you're going to pay the price for it. You're going to end up in jail. You're going to pay the price for your behaviors. You need to understand that."

We tried giving them consequences, but it was hard to find the right balance. Dealing with special-needs children while having other children that are not special-needs is tough. The punishment has to fit the crime. My biological kids would get pissed off. They were saying, "Mom, you let them get away with this, and you let them get away with that!" I would have charts and stickers and all kinds of little things that the respite nurses would tell me to try out. But you know, I had to pick and choose my battles. I don't know how I got through it.

When you're raising a bunch of adopted kids, they compare notes, so it's never just one angry at you. It's all of them angry at you because they think, *We're the adopted ones, so you're treating us different.* But William never, ever put a hand on any of them. He never hit them. He always talked to them with love and kindness. He was calm. I would be yelling, "Do you hear me? Do you hear me?" But he was always calm. He had that Godly spirit about him. He really did.

When Neil was in high school, I found out he hadn't gone to school for three weeks. He was supposed to be going to Roosevelt High School. I told Neil, "I got a letter from school saying you haven't been to school in three weeks. What's going on?" He said, "I didn't know how to tell you what's going on." I told him, "All you gotta do is just tell me." He said, "Mom, these people at school want to fight me. They're in this gang." I said, "Neil, you're over six feet tall. As tough as you are, you can stand up for yourself. I know you can fight." He said, "Mom, this guy put a gun in my face. What am I supposed to do?" That woke me up to how bad the situation was. I said, "You're not supposed to do anything. I'm getting you out of that school."

When I was a kid, I went to the same school, Roosevelt. I was there for two days, and a group of kids came into the cafeteria with chains and started beating the hell out of this Puerto Rican kid. That day, I walked out and never walked back in, so I understood exactly what my son was saying. I believed him wholeheartedly. I told him, "Neil, you don't have to go back to that school."

It turned out that while Neil was skipping school, he managed to get a little job. He was helping out this man who fixed refrigerators. He started helping the man carry the refrigerators because Neil was big and strong, and this man would give Neil a few dollars. But this was no long-term solution to the situation.

One day, I was cleaning Neil's room, and I found a gun. That was a real turning point. It was a toy gun, but it was painted to look like a real one. I told him, "Neil, if you would have had this in your pocket and went outside, you could be in real trouble. You're a big guy, but somebody could have killed you. A cop could have killed you." I took the gun and threw it onto the military base near our house. I threw it way over the fence because I didn't want Neil to climb over and get it back.

After all that went down, I did some research and found out about the Job Corps. It's a free training program for low-income teenagers that teaches them career skills so they can get a good job. Neil ended up in a training program out in Indiana for three years. He was very safe out there. He absolutely loved it, but that meant he was away from his biological father during that time. That was tough because William had just come back into our lives.

But Neil had to leave New York because I was afraid the gang members were going to kill him. They knew they couldn't beat him up. He was almost three hundred pounds and six-two, so the only thing they could do was kill him. I told William, "If they would do that to our son, can you imagine what will happen to the younger boys?" At the time, we had four young boys and three girls.

I knew it was time for a change, so our whole crew moved from New York City to South Carolina in 2002. It was easy to leave New York because I still didn't have much of a relationship with my mom. I did look out for her when the nurses went on strike at her job, and I paid the rent for her twice. I bought her clothes when my sister Mary said my mother wasn't buying any stuff for herself.

My mother had gained weight and felt very unworthy. She was attractive when she was young, but now she was thinking that you are how you look. And she didn't like the way she looked. I had to convince her that she deserved clothes. She'd say, "I don't have the money, and my rent is $800 and my check is $800." I'd say, "That's not a problem." I bought her a long leather coat, a short leather coat, boots, clothes, whatever she needed. I was making decent money, so I put some in her pocket.

One day, I told her, "Mom, I'm leaving. I'm going to South Carolina." I didn't want to tell her that William had AIDS. I told her I had to get the kids out of high school. All four boys were getting ready to go to high school, and they needed to leave before they got into trouble at the New York high schools. Otherwise, I knew they would get caught up in the gangs or something. My kids were better off coming to South Carolina than staying in New York.

That was the main reason I wanted to move to South Carolina was to keep the kids safe. New York is a difficult place. The South Bronx, the Bronx, anywhere in New York, it's hard to raise kids. The gangs are there. You could be minding your own business, and somebody will cut your face with a box cutter as you're coming down the steps from the train station. It's like an initiation to become a gang member. You have to do something horrible to get in the gang. It's ridiculous stuff that you're dealing with in New York.

The other reason I wanted to move was because William was slowly dying. I wanted my children to know their extended family. Charleston was where William came from. It's where all his extended family lives. A few members of his family went in the military. Unfortunately, some of his family is also on welfare, drinking, drugging, doing stupid things.

I came down to South Carolina a couple times before we moved. I had to find a place for us all to live, with a good school district. I was actually down there when the World Trade Center fell. It was pretty scary because I didn't know what was going on back in New York. All my kids were up there except my two youngest girls, who were with me. I was finally able to get ahold of William that day and found out everyone was safe.

I came to Charleston to buy land and do the paperwork for this double-wide trailer. Originally, the plan was to get an apartment or house, but I had eight kids and no job, so the landlords didn't want to rent to me. Somebody told me about a double-wide trailer for sale. Somebody else told me I should get a land-package deal, so that's what I did. I bought the land and the double-wide at the same time. The double-wide feels like a house. It has a real working wood fireplace. If you came in my house, you would never believe it was a double-wide.

38

We all came down to South Carolina together. William was driving a twenty-four-foot U-Haul truck, and everyone else was following behind in a blue van. But then William got sick and couldn't drive it anymore. At that time, he was walking with a cane and in a lot of pain. Neil couldn't drive the truck because we didn't have him insured to drive it.

So I had to drive the truck, but I was so short that my feet could barely reach the pedals. Believe it or not, I took William's walking cane and used it as an extension of my feet to drive the truck. I'm not kidding. I used that wooden walking cane on the gas and brake. I drove this twenty-four-foot truck with a walking cane. I know it sounds crazy, but how else were we going to get there? I took one turn really tight and felt that truck go halfway up on two wheels and come down with a bang. I was thinking, *Oh my God!*

Our life in South Carolina was very different from New York. Our road was not even paved. Every time it rained, it was muddy. My kids were from New York and used to their sneakers being very clean. So they would be walking down the road with plastic bags on their feet. My one son worked at the gas station down the road. Sometimes, he would hide in the woods alongside the road when the other kids were coming home from school. Then he would jump out and scare the living daylights out of them.

The kids weren't happy about the move, but they liked their new school, Fort Dorchester High School. To them, it felt like an Ivy League compared to what they were used to, nothing like the schools in the Bronx. There were no metal detectors. People were walking around in flip-flops. It was a totally different atmosphere. Everybody knew they were from New York. The boys had New York attitudes, and that kind of stunk. That didn't go over well. The only one who assimilated really well was Michael, my biological son. The others just thought they were big and bad because they were from New York.

When I brought my son Monty down to South Carolina, I told him, "Be careful with them white girls." He said, "What do you mean, Momma?" I said, "Boy, you need to behave with them white girls." He didn't understand that things were different in the South. Well, he's in ROTC at school, and one day, he calls me up and says, "Mom, I'm on my way home." Before I could ask if he wanted a ride, he hung up. Well, an hour later, I get a phone call telling me that the police just took Monty to jail. I said, "What?"

I go down to the police station, and they tell me this little white girl said Monty tried to rape her in the bushes behind Fort Dorchester. I'm thinking, *What? That doesn't make any sense because he just called me.* The judge told me that Monty could stay home and not go to the Department of Juvenile Justice for the next two years, but he had to wear an ankle bracelet. William and I had to sign that we would keep him under house arrest. He could not go fifty feet off the porch, and he could only go to school and church. Those charges were dropped later, but look what they did to him for all that time.

When we came down to South Carolina, my son Juan was in a residential treatment center back in New York. He begged me to get him, so I did, but I had my doubts. I said, "Well, God, let's give him another chance and see what happens." After a couple of months, he was back to the same old craziness. Then he turned eighteen and left my home. Then he came back and left again. I finally said, "No more. There's no more coming back."

Juan is bipolar. That boy took me through the mill. I can tell you stories about him. He ended up in a residential treatment center at thirteen because he wanted to sell drugs with his friends. I said, "That's not happening. I'll take you back to the judge first." I went to the principal and talked to him. We had a court hearing, and the principal told the judge what was going on. The principal told me, "There's nothing you could do to stop this except send him to a treatment center." They looked at Juan like a sociopath. Anger management programs didn't help. I've realized now that there's nothing I can do about it.

Thank God I have William. He was six foot and helped keep them all in line. I mean, Juan never did anything to me, but he would act out. I had people hold him down until the police came and took him to a hospital. It was crazy. It was insanity sometimes.

I think my boys appreciate me more now than they did when I was raising them.

39

I first visited South Carolina more than twenty years earlier when I brought Neil down as a baby to see William and his family. That was when people yelled at us in the street because I was white and he was black. Things had changed some, but I still had to think more about the racial stuff in South Carolina than when we lived in New York City.

Race has always been kind of a complicated topic for me.

My father was from Malta, and my mom was from England. People in Malta have olive-colored skin and are Mediterranean-looking. Growing up in the Bronx, I was often perceived as Puerto Rican, but I didn't identify with Puerto Rican people. Mack was black, so I was kind of acculturated into the black world because everybody in his entire family was black.

I grew up in a black world. I grew up with R&B music, Soul Train. That's how it was for those early years that I lived with my mother and Mack. It was just easy. In general, I feel closer to black people than white people. They're just more like me, and I'm more like them.

When I was younger and in foster care, one time, they sent me to a white foster home. All that family did was talk negative stuff about black people. I knew I couldn't stay there with them. My sister's black. My stepfather's black. I have black cousins. I just couldn't get with the program. I mean, if I met Kevin Costner, I'd marry him. Or Brad Pitt, I'd marry him, but there was no one like that walking around where I lived.

Most people are born into a culture, but I had to make a choice. I came into the South Bronx with a British accent and mannerisms, so I was definitely standing out. I had to pick a side. Where are you going? Who are you going to be with? Unfortunately, in 1969, that was how it was. You had to make a choice. Now I have Spanish friends. I have white friends. I have black friends.

I met most of my white friends when I was in college and in my master's program. I remember one day, we were in the group counseling class, and the whole group was white except for one person. I was sitting there, and I felt so uncomfortable. I'd never been around so many white people in my life. Since I'm basically white, you would think I would be in my element, but I felt out of place.

A lot of people, when they talk to me on the phone, if they've never met me, they expect to see a black person. This social worker called me one time and said, "Diane, I need to come and see you." And I said, "Okay," and I told her how to get there. When she knocked on the door, and I opened it, she said, "Is Diane here? Can I speak with her?" I told her, "I'm Diane." She said, "I'm sorry. I thought you were black." I said, "Why?" But I really wasn't that surprised.

In my family, color has never been an issue. I have Spanish sons. My children are biracial. I have three African American children, and it's just never been an issue. As my daughters grew up, black women were asking me, "How are you going to do your daughters' hair?" I said, "Well, I'm either going to pay somebody to do it, or I'm going to get a friend to do it." My oldest daughter, Danielle, did their hair for years, and now they do their own hair. My best friend across the street used to do their hair for me. You do what you have to do to make it work.

40

The stepdaughter who William was accused of hurting was named Daisy. Even though William went to jail, we still spent time with Daisy when we moved to South Carolina. One day, I was talking to her and said, "Sweetheart, you were just five years old when the abuse supposedly happened. You were just saying what your mother was telling you." I said, "You need to know that William never did that to you." But she refused to admit that she made it up.

God can have a wrath. I'm not saying God did what happened next, but you reap what you sow—let's just put it like that.

One day, Daisy called William and told him that this boy beat her up. At that point, Daisy was married to another man, and they had a baby together. But instead of getting her husband to help her, Daisy calls William. Even after everything that happened with him going to jail, William still looked at that girl like she was his own daughter. He had true forgiveness, so he went over to her house and tried talking to her.

Of course, no woman deserves to get beat up, but Daisy was doing things to provoke this other man further. William tried to warn her. He said, "Daisy, leave him alone. He's on probation and not stable." She said, "No, to hell with that. Blah, blah, blah."

Anyway, William left, and Daisy drove her husband to work. When she got back to the house, this other man broke into the sliding glass door. He shot her baby, and he killed her. There was one other child in the house, but he didn't shoot her. It was a three-year-old, and the police think he didn't shoot her because that was actually his sister's baby. After he shot Daisy and the baby, he laid across their bodies and killed himself.

If Daisy had not pressed his buttons, who knows what would have happened? But she told him, "I'm going to get you. You're going to jail, motherfucker. Blah, blah, blah." It's horrible what happened to Daisy and her baby, but sometimes you reap what you sow.

41

One December, when Danielle was sixteen, she kept telling me her neck hurt. I thought she was faking it because she didn't want to go to school. She would complain about this and that, and I'd say, "You're such a drama queen." But on Christmas Eve, she was in the living room with her head tilted to the right. I said, "Why are you sitting like that?" She said, "Oh, my neck hurts." She had a turtleneck on, so William said, "Let me see it." We saw a knot the size of a fist on her neck.

We took her to Saint Francis Hospital, where they admitted her right away because it was compromising her airway. They did emergency surgery, and they told me, "Thank God, everything is fine. It looks like she doesn't have cancer." I'm thinking, *Cancer? Cancer? Wait a minute. Where did that come from?* Then a week later, I get a call from the doctor. He says, "I'm sorry, it turns out that your daughter does have cancer." She had non-Hodgkin's lymphoma. I was in total shock. How do you tell your sixteen-year-old child that she has cancer?

At that point, I was taking some college classes, so William ended up taking Danielle to a lot of her doctor's appointments and chemotherapy appointments. He was there when she was throwing up a lot. I don't know if I was in denial, but it never occurred to me that she could die. She did lose her hair at one point.

Then, one night, I was watching TV. It was actually early in the morning. I can't remember the name of the show, but it was a sports show, and they were showing Andrea Jaeger, who used to be a famous tennis player. She had opened up a place in Colorado for kids with cancer. I can't remember the exact name, but it was like the Make-a-Wish Foundation.

After I saw that program, I said, "I'm going to call and tell them about Danielle." I wasn't expecting anything, but I called and got an answering machine. I left my name and everything, and a week later, a doctor called us back. He said that he wanted to learn more about Danielle. She ended up being chosen to go to Colorado for this camp. She met Kevin Costner and Cindy Crawford. I got pictures of them together. She met a lot of basketball players. She met Kenny G. I got pictures of it all. Later, Kevin Costner had them out on his ranch in the summertime.

Danielle was sixteen years old, flying around in a private jet. It sounds glamorous, but you have to remember that all these kids were possibly going to die. More than half of them did die. We used to get a newsletter from the foundation, but Danielle couldn't deal with it. She enjoyed the letter, but on the back, they would announce which kids had died. It would be fun to get the newsletter, but she knew that last page was a killer. I started ripping it off. I wouldn't let her read it. She was trying to beat the disease, but it's even harder when you keep hearing this one died and that one died.

42

The sex abuse charges against William totally bound my hands as far as marrying him. Even up to the week before he died, he wanted to marry me, but I couldn't. And it wasn't just the charges. I couldn't marry him because I was still a British citizen, so it was even more complicated.

I know that it's silly now, but part of the reason I never became an American citizen was that I was forcibly taken from England. I never wanted to leave England, and England was my original home. England was precious to me because the family I loved came from there, and I was born there. My mother married Mack, an American, but because she never got her citizenship, I never became a US citizen.

Now they've changed the laws, so it would be easier to become a US citizen than it was in the past. I've thought about it. I can't get Social Security unless I become a citizen. Also, I can't work any state jobs unless I'm a citizen, so that's another reason I need to go ahead and do that. But it costs $650, and I'm always saying, "I'll do it next year. I'll do it next year."

During the 2008 election, when Obama was running, my pastor said, "Diane, you didn't vote?" I told him, "No, I can't because I'm not an American citizen." They were pissed at me, but I said, "Well, I got eight kids who will vote!"

I took care of William for eleven years before he passed, but God gave us favor during that time. William had AIDS. Then, he got pancreatic cancer. He had type 1 diabetes. He had skin cancer. He had things that should have taken him out, but he would say to those doctors, "Greater is He that lives in me than he that's in the world."

William and I were best friends. We did everything together. We spent eighteen hours of the day together most of the time. I was an at-home mom, and he was at home too. He did work, but he worked the overnight shift, so we spent a lot of time with each other and enjoyed our time together. We enjoyed each other's company immensely and hardly ever fought. If we did, it was like a couple of minutes, and it never lasted into the next day.

There was just one time he went away for the entire day after an argument. It was six weeks before he died. I guess I was angry, and I knew he was dying. I was trying to give him what he wanted, but I was just tired. He had some life insurance, and he went to get some more. He said, "Diane, I put my sister on my life insurance also." When I heard that, I'm saying to myself, *This life insurance doesn't mean anything because the end is near, and they're not going to pay out anything.* But I understood that he was trying to protect me. When he told me about his sister being on this new policy, I said, "I don't care," but he misunderstood me. He responded to me, "You don't care? Now you don't care?" Anyway, we ended up apart that day. I was thinking, *This is stupid. I may not have him in a few weeks, but he is here now.* Then I thought, *Well, he needs to visit his sister and cousins and nephews. Let them have that moment and let me have some downtime.*

Due to all his health conditions, he should have died a lot earlier, but God gave him favor. The way he died was amazing because he worked up until two weeks before he died. When he was really sick, he urinated in our bed. That was when I knew something was wrong. I looked, and his eyes were half open. I took him to Trident Hospital. The nurse looked at everything he had wrong with him and said, "My God. It's amazing he's still alive." That's what's she told me, and I said, "What are you saying? Are you telling me he's about to die?" They transferred him to a bigger hospital, and then they put him in hospice.

He ended up coming back to our home for the final week. I decided to bring everybody, even his ex-wife, to see him. I let even her come and say goodbye to him because she had three of his children.

After he died, she kissed him in his coffin. People looked at me and said, "You let her do that?" Yeah, I did. You know why? Because I want everybody to know she lied about the sex abuse charges. If you were there and saw her kiss William in his coffin, you would know those charges weren't true. You would be thinking, *It's the classic situation.* People do horrible things to each other when getting a divorce, and that's what it was.

When William was dying at home, Cora was eleven, and Carrie was fourteen. All he kept saying was "Take care of my girls. Promise, promise, promise." He had everybody promising to take care of his girls. He loved them, and they loved him.

The girls still live in that same home where he died, and it's very difficult for them. We've painted, and we've bought new furniture. We've changed things around, but I know that when they come into my bedroom, they still know he died in that room. There's still pain because that's where he died. After he died, everybody was going into the room to say goodbye. Everybody went in there one by one. Carrie refused to go in, but Cora laid on the bed with him under his arm for a while. She was just eleven.

When I lost William, I lost so much: our retirement, our dreams, our planned vacations. There were so many secondary losses—him walking our kids down the aisle, him seeing his grandkids. Nobody gave money for the funeral except his brother's wife. She gave me a thousand dollars. His brother, Julius, died two years before, and his wife gave me a thousand dollars from one of those penny policies his mother had. But other than that, I had to get a loan against my house to bury William. I did what I had to do.

Will, my ex, and his new wife actually came to William's funeral. Why would my ex-husband, the father of my two kids, come to William's funeral? Because he really respected William. After we split up, Will eventually started getting himself together. Every time he wanted to come be with the kids, I let him as long as I knew he was clean. I let him take them to Florida. I let him take them to his parents. I never stopped him from being a parent. I never went after Will for child support because William took such good care of us.

We have this one client now in our counseling program. He's just finding out that he's dying, and he's in his forties, and he's got teenagers. My advice to him was that he not choose to die at home. I know you don't want to die in the hospital. I get that, but you don't want to die at home. I think maybe hospice could be in your house, but when it gets really, really bad, I think then they should move you. Maybe rent a little cottage nearby or something where everybody could be around, but it's not in a hospital environment.

That way, at least when you go home, you don't have the memory of them wheeling the dead body out. That's what my kids saw. Right after Christmas, they saw their dad being wheeled out, so it's hard for them. The memories are not as hard for me. I don't really think about him dead in our bedroom. I know he loved me, so I don't have any pain about that. But for the kids' sake, it would be better to have the actual death happen someplace else—so they don't have to remember their dad died in this room.

43

What really hurt me when William died was that I had no real support system. I felt like I was on my own, but I also had to be supporting all my kids. I didn't know about any free counseling anywhere. There was a grief support group offered to me through hospice, but when I went to that group, everybody looked like they were ninety years old. I just didn't feel the connection. These people had these long, wonderful marriages, and then there was me, so I didn't continue to go.

In the months after William died, I just tried to work myself to death. I tried not to deal with anything. My daughters were hurting really bad, but I just stuffed up all my emotions. I ate my emotions—let's put it like that. Sometimes, I stayed in Applebee's all night long, drinking coffee, and I just ate my emotions. Then, one day, I felt this rush in my lips, like a freezing kind of thing. My lips were numb, and I knew something was wrong. I went in the bathroom, and the right side of my face had fallen.

I called Danielle and told her that I thought I was having a stroke. She went on the internet to see if she could find any information. She said, "Mama, can you move your hand?" And I said, "Yeah." She said, "Can you move your toes?" I said, "Yeah." She said, "You're not having a stroke, but I'm coming over right now to take you to the hospital."

She took me to the emergency room, and they thought I was having a stroke. At that point, I was like 280 pounds. They took me to the cardiovascular department at MUSC, and they did the stress test and all that. It turns out, it wasn't a stroke. They told me I had Bell's palsy. I said, "What in the world? What's Bell's palsy?" They explained that it's when half of your face gets paralyzed, and it should eventually clear up on its own.

When I was down in the hospital that night, I slept like an elephant. I couldn't sleep in my bedroom at home, but I was exhausted all the time. I was telling myself that it didn't bother me that William died in that room, but emotionally, I couldn't bear it.

In addition to Bell's palsy, I developed aphasia. I had slurred speech for a year. You can still see the effects of the Bell's palsy. If you look at my eyes, they're not symmetrical anymore. They used to be perfectly symmetrical, but the right one is now a little smaller. It closes when I'm really tired.

The next day in the hospital, a doctor came to give me an update on all the tests. He said my cholesterol levels were great because I didn't eat a lot of fried food. He said, "You also have type 2 diabetes," which I already knew. He said, "There's absolutely nothing wrong with your heart. It's your soul that's in trouble." He told me, "I can fix a sick heart, but I cannot fix a sick soul. You need to get some help." He told me I could die if I continued in the same direction. He said, "If you don't reach out and get some help, you will die."

I didn't think doctors were supposed to talk that way, but I guess this guy was a Christian. I don't know why he was speaking to me that frankly, but he said, "You need to get some kind of help, whether it's counseling or clergy." I took what he said seriously.

When I went home from the hospital, I turned to God that night. There were so many times in my life when I was always running away from God. I was so mad at Him for everything that went on when I was a child, from the molestation to all the physical abuse. I was also mad at God for giving me William and then taking him away from me. That night, when I went home, I was on my knees in the living room. I was yelling at God, telling him how mad

I was. Then I started crying and asking Him to help me.

Within twenty-four hours, Danielle brought this lady to my house named Nora.

My daughter had been in a restaurant earlier that day, and she heard two people talking about God. She said, "Excuse me, but can I talk to you for a minute?" She said, "I don't mean to interrupt your dinner, but my stepfather just died. My mom has got Bell's palsy, and I don't think my mom is going to make it." She just went and told them everything about me.

That day, Nora came home with Danielle. I was lying on the couch, and she said, "Hello." And I said, "Hi." She told me, "I want to invite you to our church," and I said, "No, that's okay." Now remember that less than twenty-four hours earlier, I was on my knees asking God to help me, but now I'm thinking, *No, that's okay. I don't need your church. I'll just lie here on the couch.*

Well, Nora didn't take no for an answer. She had lost her father, so she had some sense of what my kids were going through. She took my youngest daughter, Cora, with her for three days to give her some support. Then she invited me to church again, and I said, "No, thank you." Well, Danielle said, "Mom, please just go one time. Do it for me." So I did. I went one time. I guess the church knew I was coming with my family because they had chairs set up in a circle after the Bible study.

They talked to us for a little while and then asked if we would come back the next day because they were doing a revival. I said, "Yeah, okay." At that revival, something moved in my spirit. Something connected. My spirit connected with the Holy Spirit in that church. That's what I believe.

At the revival, they just started calling up families. Well, as they were doing that, I realized that my family wasn't the only one having problems. The pastor must have called up about six different families. So then I start thinking, *Okay, Diane, are you gonna let go of this? Are you gonna let God take over? What are you gonna do?* And I determined in my mind that no matter what, I'm gonna be happy. This is what the Holy Spirit put in my heart.

I said to myself, "If I only had a week of life left, what would I want to do? What would I do?" And I've tried to keep that attitude since then. When all the little trials and tribulations keep coming in my mind, I just pretend like I only got a week left of life. I refuse to acknowledge the craziness. That's it. I just refuse to acknowledge it.

After the revival, the pastor touched my cheek because my face was still dropped from the Bell's palsy, and he told me he could see my smile. Now, he calls me "Shorty," but he used to call me "Miss D." He was very kind, and he told me my life was not over.

The grass at my house was so overgrown because I wasn't taking care of anything, and one day, I hear this noise in my yard. I look out, and I see that the pastor had come to my house to cut my grass. I couldn't believe it. He's an important figure in the church, and it's really hot out there. But there he is with his lawnmower. He's got this little wet rag on his head, and he's saying, "Don't pay this little black man no mind." I tell him, "You don't have to do that," and he says, "I know, but I want to."

When the pastor and his family first met us, they were on the way to Puerto Rico for vacation. When he got down there, he sent me a text saying, "How are you and the girls? Just thinking about you." When he got back, he said, "Miss D, did you get my text?" I said, "Yes, I did get that text." He said, "Why didn't you return it?" I told him I didn't know how to send a text, and he said, "Oh, well, you're going to learn now," and he made me text him every day until I got the hang of it.

Over time, the church became a bigger and bigger part of my life. It gave me strength during challenging times. I had two car accidents because I was exhausted. I was still grieving William and working myself to death. I totaled the car twice, but I walked away both times with just scratches, nothing serious. God was looking out for me.

I started taking theology classes to learn more about God. After the accidents, my pastor said, "I can't let you continue to take these classes. You're working yourself too hard." I was upset, and I said, "So you're going to take God away from me? You're really going to do this?" And he said, "Diane, it's just not the right time right now."

As I look back, he was definitely right. I needed to take that break, but I wasn't done studying. Eventually, I decided to go back to school and get my master's degree in counseling. It was some hard work, but I'm so glad I took that step.

It wasn't until I returned to church that I learned about Genesis and that God gives us free will. But when we get free will, it can be dangerous. Then I realized it wasn't God who beat me when I was young. It wasn't God who molested me. It wasn't God who did all the horrible things to me. It was people like Mack who God gave free will to. God's not happy about what happened to me, but he did put all those angels in my path.

My life started to make sense. I learned how to take the negative things out of my mind and put new, positive things in my mind instead.

I would try taking the kids to church. I didn't want to beat them over the head with church, but I wanted them to know God. I want them to realize that there's a higher power out there, and you have to determine how you want to live your life and what you can learn. You have to determine that you want to be happy. No matter your circumstances, you have to determine how to move forward.

I could sit here and say, "Woe is me. My son got arrested last week. Oh, poor me, my daughter is sick." Or, I can say, "You know what? Get up and learn from this experience. Don't let it define you. Let's go forward." Sometimes, you just need to make the best of it. You know what I mean? Because if you don't, you will just get caught up in the chaos.

Diane, age 51

44

During this period of my life, I had really distanced myself from my mother and my sister Mary. I needed to do that for my own emotional wellbeing, and I was fine with that. Or I thought I was.

As I look back on our childhood, I feel like Mary was given everything growing up, or at least a lot more than me. But I think somehow, in her mind, she blamed herself for the abuse that my brother and I suffered. In some ways, she could have been the perfect child, but it seems like she decided to do everything not to be perfect. She became an alcoholic. She became a drug addict.

She got arrested for a DWI, and she went to live with my mother. They put Mary on probation, but she didn't have an apartment in her name, so that's why she had to move in with my mom. From the time she moved in, she was horrible to her, from what my mother says. Mary was being very manipulative.

After Mary moved in, she manipulated her husband into living there also. He is a stone-cold drug addict. They did a lot of yelling, screaming, arguing. She'd be nice to my mother to get her monthly pension check, but then once the money was gone, she'd be saying horrible, mean things to her like, "Your life is over. Don't bother me. You had your life. Now let me have mine." I mean, the worst things to say to somebody.

It got to the point where my mother had a little hamster in her room, and that was her only friend. That's who she would talk to every day. His name was Mr. Jingles. He was a rodent, no better than a rat. How sad is that? That the only person you have to talk to for months and months is a rat? My mom would just go and stay in her room. She was miserable. She was fragile and psychologically tormented by my sister.

Around this time, my mom started calling my daughter, Danielle. Sometimes, she was talking to her three hours a day on the phone, but my daughter wasn't telling me any of this. Then, one day, my daughter started making these suggestions, saying, "How would you like it if Grandma came to visit us?" And I tried to ignore her, saying, "I'm busy right now. I don't want to talk about it."

I had learned to cut myself off emotionally from my mother. As an adult, when I would visit her, she'd often say, "What the hell are you doing here?" You can only say that to somebody so many times before they start thinking, *Okay, I get it*. We lived in the same area of New York, just fifteen minutes away from each other, and we wouldn't see each other for over a year. I came to terms with the fact that she would never be the mother I wanted. I had moved on, and I buried her in my mind.

But my daughter kept making hints about my mother coming to visit us, and I said, "Well, I don't care if she comes for a couple of weeks. I can deal with that." And then my daughter said, "How would you like it if Grandma actually came to live with us?" I said, "I wouldn't like it at all. Why would I like that?" The mother I knew yelled and screamed. She's horrible. She's vulgar-mouthed, and I didn't want that in my house.

45

In eleven years, I'd seen my mother twice, for two weeks total. The idea of her coming to visit was okay, but I never expected her to actually live with me. I didn't see that coming. I was very blindsided. To be fair, she came to visit not knowing that she wanted to stay because she had no idea herself. All she knew was that she was miserable living with my sister, so she came to South Carolina.

When I first saw her, she was no longer my middle-aged mother. She was an old woman. She was seventy-six but looked older because of everything she'd gone through. After she had been staying with me for a few days, she told me she couldn't go back to live with my sister. She was being emotionally abused by Mary and her alcoholic, drug-addict husband.

I don't know what happened or what I was thinking, but I agreed to let her stay. I told her she could move in with me, but I didn't realize what that meant for me. I had buried her in my mind. That's what you have to do when your mother doesn't want you for all those years. Christmas, Thanksgiving, Easter—I would always be at somebody else's house. When I was younger, counselors would take pity on me and take me to their houses, but I never felt like I belonged because I wasn't part of that family. It was somebody else's family. That was really, really difficult for me.

But eventually, I learned how to let that go. There's a scripture in the Bible that says something like, "Hate your mother and father and follow me." Well, God doesn't really want you to hate your mother and father. What He's saying is if your parents don't follow Him, you need to abandon them and follow Him. That's what I tried to do. In my mind, I buried my mother because she was never going to be the mother every child wants a mother to be.

Now that she was living with me, we had to get to know each other all over again. She changed dramatically from what she used to be. One night, we were watching a movie called *Antwone Fisher*. It's about a kid who suffers horrible verbal, physical, and sexual abuse. As we're watching, she goes, "Oh, my gosh, that's so horrible. How could anyone do that to a child?" I was stunned. I'm thinking, *Really? Really?* I'm looking at the scars on my arms. *You don't remember anything you did to me?* I didn't say anything even though I was tempted. She was actually crying while watching the movie.

When I was growing up, my mother never said she loved me. Now that she was living with me, she started kissing me every night before she went to bed. Never when I was a kid did she kiss me. I don't remember her ever kissing me. I don't remember her ever saying she loved me.

I decided that the only thing my mom could do was become a better grandmother to my kids. I told her, "You have a grandson who's thirty-nine years old. You need to connect with him and start talking to him. If you want to make peace with me, you need to reach out to my kids, your grandkids, and be a good grandma to them. That's how you make it right." I look at my girls and boys, all eight of them. Had my life not gone the way it went, I would not have those children today. I love them all.

There were other challenges. I didn't realize my mother did not understand boundaries. I couldn't study at home when she was there, so I'd have to go to church or the library. One night, I was exhausted. I came in at 1 a.m., and she said, "Don't you want to watch TV with me?" I don't like to watch TV. I like to read. But she doesn't know what I like because she hasn't known me since I was fourteen.

I bought her coats because she needed them. I know how to be a daughter. I know how to take care of family, but then there's that part of me thinking, *I just buried my husband a couple of years ago, and that was a long, terminal illness. Watching him decline in health was really tough. I'm not ready to go through that all again with her.*

My pastor said, "Diane, do you have a doctor for your mother?" I looked at him and said, "Pastor, you have to understand, my mother came to me an old lady. I don't know anything about senior citizens at all." So I had to research this stuff and get her a primary caregiver and all that stuff. I really resented it at times.

I resented it because I felt it just wasn't fair. She spends all these years with other people and neglects my family completely, and now I'm supposed to take care of her into her old age until she dies? I wonder if I'll ever let go of that resentment completely, to be honest with you.

Sharon, age 76

46

When she first started living with me, my mom would struggle because she wanted to be in control. I told her, "You cannot control anybody but yourself. If you try to control other people, you're only going to lead yourself into frustration." And that's what happened. One night, she got frustrated over something minor, and she said, "Pack my clothes. I want to leave." I said, "I'm not packing your clothes. I didn't unpack them for you. If you want to leave, you pack them." I stayed very calm. I wasn't screaming and yelling. I said, "If you want to pack your clothes and leave, then tell me where you're going, and I'll make sure you get there." She quieted down after that.

She got upset sometimes with my daughters. They were sixteen and nineteen. She'd say, "They don't tell me what they're doing. They don't tell me where they're going." My girls were actually very nice to her. I said, "Mom, these are your grandchildren, and you've only known them for seven weeks. You should have been in their life since they came to live with me." You can't expect to have this instant relationship. I said, "They respect you. They do your hair. They like you, but they're not going to share intimate details with you right now. They're not going to ask you if they can do this or that. They're just not going to do it."

My mom was used to the chaos with Mary and husband—the drama of arguments all around her. Living in my house was a big change. My house is quiet, peaceful. One time, she said, "I was afraid last night." I said, "You're afraid? Afraid of what? I have bars on my windows. How are you afraid? Nobody can get in here. You have a telephone and a phone book. If you're lonely or scared, you have to pick up the phone and call somebody." I said, "You have to learn how to be all right by yourself."

We all have to learn that. There are times when we are going to be alone. We're not going to have that connectedness with somebody. Maybe our spouse died, like mine, or maybe you don't have a boyfriend or whatever. Sometimes you just don't have that connectedness. You have to connect yourself with God and stay in the spirit.

I like being with me. I'm comfortable with me. I think many people don't realize that there will be times in your life when you have to learn how to be alone. If you have a spiritual life, then you know you're not totally alone. You know God is always with you. You have to be okay with you. If you don't like yourself, then who's going to like you?

After my mom moved in, Mary didn't call her. My mother was upset about that. She didn't understand that manipulating your children with your money makes them dependent on you. If they're dependent on you, then you get them stuck, so they can't fully develop in their lives.

In many ways, I think my mom knew exactly what she was doing with Mary. She said she didn't, but I think she did. By enabling them with her money, she made them dysfunctional, unable to get out and stand on their own. I told her, "By staying with me, you have dis-enabled them. Now they're a hot mess, and you're pissed off because they're not calling you. You need to realize that nothing but your money kept that whole thing going."

Her moving into my house was such a big adjustment. I was dealing with a mother who I couldn't stand for most of my life. One day, I realized I needed to be more honest with her about my past feelings. I said, "When you called me in the past, sometimes I didn't answer the phone. I just didn't want to talk to you. I'm sorry." I said,

"Many times, I didn't answer the phone because all you wanted to talk about was Mary and her family. I was sick and tired of it. I had to protect myself, so I just wouldn't answer the phone." When I did pick up, I would talk to her maybe ten minutes. Then I would make an excuse to get off the phone. I'd say, "Mom, I got to go to work."

I had carved out a new life in South Carolina. Now, suddenly, she is in my house. I was telling my friends, "I'm living with my mother again," and they all went, "Uh-uh. No. You got it backward. *She's* living with *you*. Remember that." I'm thinking, *Yeah, you're right.* I had to get my mother to understand: "I don't live with *you*. You live with *me*."

After she moved to South Carolina, she didn't want to get her own apartment. She got a good pension and could definitely afford a nice apartment. For the rest of her life, she was in good shape financially. She gets about $3,500 a month until she dies. But she said, "No, I don't want to get my own apartment. I want to be with you. I want to live with you and help you."

Part of me knew I needed the help because I was a struggling student, but the other part didn't want it. And another said, *Well, damn, she does owe me.* I'm a counselor. I knew what to say to psychologically manipulate her. I could have her right where I want her, but the Holy Spirit would not let me. Two wrongs don't make a right.

I had to make a lot of changes to having a senior citizen in my home. The mother that showed up on my doorstep could barely walk. She was shaky, and her feet were swollen. My sister had not taken care of her at all. She needed a walker. After a while, she didn't need a walker anymore because I walked with her and was active with her.

One day, she got sick. She came to my room at 7 a.m. to wake me up. She said, "I don't feel well, Diane. I'm going to go lie down." I was thinking, *Wow, what's wrong?* I felt sorry for her. I didn't want to feel sorry for her, but I did. So I helped her back into bed. After I went to work, I called my daughter, asking, "How's she doing?" She told me, "She's sleeping. She's doing okay. She ate some soup." I was thinking, *God is trying to tell me something.* He's telling me, "Look, your mom is seventy-six. Get it together. Either you're going to let her back into your life, or you're not. Don't keep punishing her." That day, I really turned a corner with my mom.

She wanted me to love her. She'd go, "Diane, I love you, even though I know you don't believe me." That was a lot to take in, but I didn't say anything. She leaned in to kiss me before bed. I wanted to grab her wrist and say, "No, leave me alone," but I let her kiss me because she'd changed. At least, I believed that she believed she had changed.

It was very stressful for me because she wanted to be around me all the time. I wanted her to leave me alone when I came home from work. I wanted to put my candles on and go in my room. I wanted quiet time and didn't want to talk to her. When we watched the news, she repeated everything. The TV announcer would say, "President Obama did this," and she'd say, "Diane, President Obama did this," like an echo. *God, give me the patience.*

47

I started taking her to my church on Sunday. After a few months, she told me she was finally ready to turn to God. I told her, "Mom, God was always there. You just had your back to him. When you finally decided that you couldn't take your life with Mary, you finally looked toward God. God answered you as soon as you looked toward Him."

At my church, she was just having a ball. I was glad at first, but then I started getting angry. I was feeling kind of left out. I was thinking, *Wow! This church has been my family and life, and now it's becoming her life. The ladies in the church seem to be more worried about her than they are about me.* I guess the ladies knew I was in a good place with Christ. Maybe they felt it was important to turn some attention to my mom since my sister had paid her no attention.

But I admit I was jealous because the older women had mothered me for years. Now they became her friends and gave her their attention. I had called them my "moms." I didn't want them to be her friend because I wanted them to keep being my moms. I know that sounds very little-girlish, but my emotions got thrown up in the air like tossed salad. My pastor was telling my mom, "You are saved, and all is forgiven. Write everything down that you regret. Then burn it and never look at it again because God forgives you." I said, "Well, God may forgive her, but what about me? Am I just supposed to turn the other cheek?"

I know how to be a daughter. Taking care of her physically was the easy part. It's the emotional part that gets in the way. I admitted this to my pastor, and she told me, "Diane, you need to tell your mother how you're feeling." I went home and told my mom, "I am jealous of you. I'm jealous that you came here and took over my world. Now you're right smack in the middle of my world. The ladies at church were my spiritual friends, and now you're calling them 'Father' and 'Mama B.'" She listened, but I'm not sure she understood what I was trying to convey.

One day, I came home from work, and she had a blanket on her legs. When she got up to go to bed, she moved the blanket, and I could see something was wrong. I said, "What happened to your legs? They're so swollen." I said, "We gotta go to the emergency room." It's after 10, but it turned out she wasn't taking her medicine.

The doctor said she needed to stay off her feet for a week. After we got back from the hospital, she said, "Oh, I have to get a note for the pastor." I said, "Why?" She said, "I have to show him why I can't go to church on Sunday." I said, "No, you don't. What are you talking about?" She was thinking like a little kid. I said, "You are freaking embarrassing me. You don't have to give a note to a pastor. You've got your independent life."

I'm protective of her because she is my mom, but it's really hard to live with her. I tried not to hold any animosity toward her. I tried to remember that she didn't have any positive role models in her life when she was growing up because she didn't have any family. When she was working as a prostitute, she was having sex with her johns many times a day. That couldn't have been fun. I'm sure that that messed with her psyche.

In some ways, she's childlike, looking for affirmation. I pray to God, "Give me patience." *I just took care of a man I loved dearly for eleven years and had to watch him die, and now here my mom is wearing Poise Pads. When will she be wearing Depends?* Do I really want to do this? And why should I be the one taking care of you after you treated me like dirt? You beat the hell out of me and allowed your husband to do things to me that I don't even want to remember. Why should I? Why should I?

As my mom lived with me, she grew to understand how important William was to me. She loved him despite not spending much time with him when he was alive. She never came to support me after he died. She was never there for me. But now she realizes he's really gone. She grieved his loss and wanted to buy a tombstone for him. She wanted to cut the grass on his grave and make it nice. That meant something. She was trying.

After my mom had been living with me for a while, she started talking to my sister Mary again, saying, "Diane has been nothing but nice to me." And that was true because I am who I am. Two wrongs don't make a right, and I decided I wasn't going to hurt her the way she hurt me. That pain is too awful and it's not the example I want to set for my daughters. I know my daughters are watching me. My son is watching me. Everybody is watching me to see how I do with my mother back in my life. And to be honest, when I get up in age, I hope they treat me the way I'm treating my mom.

I have to model it. God would not be pleased if I treated my mother wrongly. No matter what happened, she gave me the breath of life. No matter what she did to me, she brought me into the world. She could have aborted me. I could have been in a toilet somewhere. She did try to kill me as a baby. She put me in front of the gas oven, along with David, but she also put herself in front of that oven.

48

One day, Mary says, "Oh, you just wait and see. The real Sharon is going to show up one day." At that point, my mom had been with me about three months, and things were going okay. So I didn't pay attention to what Mary was saying.

Well, a few weeks later, the real Sharon did show up one Sunday in church. I was at a table paying the tithes for my mother and me. I put our offerings in separate envelopes. While I'm doing this, I didn't realize my mom was talking to the pastor. Later, I find out that my mother told the pastor, "I only have a dollar because Diane has my bank card, and she didn't take me to the bank to get any money out. This is all I can give today." It made me look horrible, but I actually had her offerings with me. I had been out late the night before and forgot to tell her I went to the bank. I always gave her money for the offerings. But my mom was so quick to blame me in front of the pastors. I felt like she deliberately wanted to make me look bad.

My pastor called me over and said, "Diane, you have something that belongs to your mother." I felt like I was being rebuked, thinking, *Wait a minute. I'm fifty-three years old. Why are you asking me this?* I didn't say this out loud because I respect my pastors. They've helped me come a long way in my work with Christ. They helped me heal over William and helped me with my daughters. I do really respect them, but I was irritated at being confronted like this.

My pastor goes, "Don't you have something that belongs to your mother?" I'm confused and ask, "Something that belongs to my mother? No, not that I know of." And my pastor goes, "Don't you have her bank card?" The way my pastor looked at me, I felt like that nine-year-old kid again. I felt like my mother was trying to take away my integrity in the church. It was like a pimple that had not been treated and turned into a huge boil.

At that point, I blew up. The boil had burst, and the stench was everywhere. I reacted, and I yelled, "What are you trying to do?" I stormed out of the church. My pastor came behind me, and I told her, "You can have my mother." I meant it. I was crying. I was bawling. I was so upset because I felt like my mother had come back into my life and taken over everything that was precious to me. I found her card and walked back in with it. I told the pastor, "Here's her bank card," and she said, "Okay, give it to your mother." I said, "No! You give it to her," and threw it on the table. I said, "You give it to her," and stormed out.

Now I'm crying even more. Another pastor is trying to comfort me, and I feel awful, horrible, because the pastor had nothing to do with it. My mother set me up for embarrassment and failure. My sister's voice kept going in my ear, "You'll see. The real Sharon will show up."

Then my mother came into the lobby and goes, "Well, I don't give a damn about them anyway." And I think, *No, you don't give a damn because you've only been here three months.* I said, "You don't have the connectedness and belongingness and relationships that I have with everybody in the church. You're just enjoying the attention."

I was devastated, upset about how I allowed my mom to make me angry. I know how to think like Christ. Normally, when my mother would say something that bothered me, I would think, *Take a breath. What would Jesus do?* But that day, I was caught off guard. God in His infinite wisdom said, "Okay, I'm going to take your old mother out of the grave. You thought you put her in the grave and buried her, but I'm going to resurrect her whether you like it or not. I'm going to make you deal with this mess."

So that is what He did.

It was just me and my mom outside the church. The church service was beginning, and people were walking in. I had just gone flying out the door, going crazy. I lost it. As they say, I fell. I fell hard. I cried for two days—literally. It wasn't a teardrop. It was running water down my cheeks.

At one point, I finally came to my senses. I realized my mom and I could only move forward and make new memories. I couldn't hold on to all my past anger toward her. *I have to let the anger go.* I realized later that I ended up letting go of all that old resentment in church that day. I guess God felt that that was the safest place for me to do it. I think God was saying to me, "You think you're pretty slick. You know my Word. You say, 'How would God answer my mother?'"

I had tried to stay calm, but God blindsided me. He blindsided me, and He let my mother show a part of her old self that just made me erupt.

49

After my eruption at church, I got sent down at my church. That meant I couldn't be an usher for a while. That broke my heart. You have no idea how painful that was for me because I take working for the Lord seriously. After our prayer group that week, I went up to my pastor and said, "Please just give me a couple of minutes." He said, "You can have more than a couple of minutes, Diane," and I just started crying.

I told my pastor, "I'm so jealous. You take my mom everywhere. You do everything for her. I'm so jealous." I was like that little kid again. I finally got this family at my church that I belonged to, but my mother had to come and mess that up for me. I didn't realize that I actually messed it up for myself. I should have gone to them and told them how I was feeling, but I didn't. Lesson learned. Even though I was fifty-three years old, when dealing with my mother, it's easy to be that child again—very easy.

I was upset with the pastors. I said, "I'm hurt." I was crying, and they were looking at me. I started telling them what was in my heart. I pulled my sleeves up and said, "Do you see the scar right here? That's from my mom." I showed them my tooth, which is a cap from when my mother hit me in the mouth with a frying pan. Then my pastor—he's so funny, and that's what I love about him because he makes me laugh—pulls out his lip and shows me his own bad tooth, and he says, "Yeah, I can relate." But I told him, "No, I want to be the victim right now. I don't want you to make me laugh." But that's what he did, and that's what I love about him.

My pastors were very understanding once we talked, but I was not happy with my behavior. I should have known it had to happen at some point. I just didn't know it was going to happen in church.

After everything went down, my mother's first comment was "Well, I'm not going to go back to that church because it's going to be embarrassing. Everyone will see you sitting down rather than ushering." I told her, "Well, you can stay home if you want, but I am going to church." I didn't care what anybody in the congregation thought. My relationship is with God. Yes, I did disrespect my leaders. I didn't mean to. I know they weren't at fault. I felt like I defiled the church with my hatred of my mother's behavior. I just felt so much remorse about it. Eventually, she decided to go back with me.

Afterward, I talked about the incident with my son, Neil. My mother never had a relationship with him, but he knew everything about her. He said, "Mom, I understand what you're saying. My skin is pretty thick when it comes to grandma." He said, "But I'm realizing that I have to forgive her."

He's a man of God. My son's not a pastor, but he's a man of God, and I said, "Well, Neil, when I go to church on Sunday, I'm not going to sit in the pews. I've been doing this usher thing for so long. I'm going to go up to the side, and I'm going to stand even though I can't usher." And Neil said, "No, Mom, you need to sit next to her."

I said, "Neil, really?" He said, "Yes, you need to sit next to her. I know that's hard because I know how you feel right now, but you need to be the bigger person." So I sat next to her, but when the sermon came, I stood—because I always did. Otherwise, I was next to her.

I'm realizing that for me to be a good, effective counselor, I have to work on what's going on with me and her first. My mother has apologized to me over and over again. She says, "I'm sorry," but she doesn't say what she's sorry for. I know in my heart that she knows. I just have to accept her general "I'm sorry" and move on.

I really believe that part of the problem between her and me is that I constantly remind her of my biological father, her old pimp from London. I think a lot of her anger that came out on me was really meant for him. That's what I think. I don't think she ever wanted me as a baby. She never told me whether she did or didn't. I just assume she didn't because of the way she treated me. She never said she loved me. I felt like I was always a problem for her.

And it's difficult for me because I felt I was taken away from my real family. That's the hard part. She may be my biological mom, but my real mom? That's Carolyn Hart. She dead now, but she was my mom. She's the one I called Mommy when I was growing up. She is the one who mothered me, nurtured me, and loved me unconditionally. But she's gone now. And here comes my biological mother back into my life. I feel like God is giving us another chance. I guess God had to take my mother through some storms first for her to fully realize what she had done to me.

One day, my pastor asked me, "Diane, do you believe your mother has changed?" I said, "Yes, I do believe she changed. I believe she had to go through some stuff with my sister, some really bad stuff, for a lot of years, to realize the error of her ways. I do believe she has remorse, and I am trying desperately to forgive her." Have I forgiven her 100 percent? I wish I could say, "Yes," but every time my anger wells up, I say, "God help me with this. Help me with this."

I just try to focus on moving forward. I told her, "Mom, we are making new memories." A couple of times, she's flipped out on me, and I just asked, "Mom, what's going on? What's the matter?" I let her tell me and get it off her chest. Then I say, "All right, well, that's not a big problem. Just calm down for a minute." I know God is trying to show me how I can forgive her. If I can show other people that I can forgive her and allow her back into my life, then I feel like it's all been worth it in the long run. I want people to know that nothing's impossible with God in your life. Nothing is impossible.

In many ways, I believe she is redeemed. I know it sounds crazy, but I believe she's my best friend now. I certainly never thought I'd ever say those words, but that's how I feel. I would say God is my right arm, and my mom is my left right now.

She knows about this book, and she does not want to be a part of it. I explained that she doesn't have to read the book. I told her, "No one will make you read it." But I'm just telling our history together. It is what it is. And if telling my story can help somebody else, then that's what the purpose is.

50

I'm very into church, and I love God, but I only agree with some things up to a certain point. One of those rules is not having sex before you're married. I agree with that if you're a teenager, but if you've already been married for many years, things are different. When you're fifty-three, it's hard to meet people.

Well, one day, I met somebody who got my attention. And you're not going to believe it, but his name is William also. I guess that makes him William 3.

I'd known William for over a year. I was completing my master's degree and working in the counseling department at a local public school. William worked at the same school and was the head of the custodial management department. He ran the cleaning crew.

He seemed like a very nice fellow, and he kept giving me his business card with his phone number on it. He said, "You're going to school all the time, Diane. You need to have fun once in a while." One time, he tried to get me to go out with him, and I said, "You're a distraction. I need to finish what I'm doing." But he kept saying, "When are you going to let me take you to the movies? When are you going to let me do this? When are you going to let me do that?" Each time he saw me, he told me, "I bet you lost my card again," and he would give me another. He must have given me nine of his business cards.

One day, I'm sitting in the break room at school, talking to my girlfriend. William walks up behind me, and he puts his card down on the table. This is probably the tenth time. I looked at him and said, "Oh, I'm sorry, I was going to call you." I honestly did think about calling him, but then I'd think, *I've got this book to read for my classes. If I talk to him, he's not going to let me get off the phone.* This time, he gives me a pen and turns over his business card. He says, "Write down your number. I'm tired of waiting for you to call me." So I wrote down my number, and he left. Then it went out of my head, and I wasn't thinking about it anymore.

Well, about 1 a.m., he sends me a text that says, "Are you still up? I just got home." He works a second job at night. I text him, "Yeah, I'm awake," so we started talking on the phone. He said, "Diane, I know that you know that I like you. I've been liking you for a long time." I said, "Okay, I know that, but I also see you walk other women to their cars all the time." He told me, "I'm just a nice guy like that. I'm just carrying teachers' stuff for them." That may be true, but I told him, "Look, you have the same name as my two husbands, and that really bothers me." So then he said, "Well, you can call me Red instead. That's what some people call me." I said, "Okay. That's what I'll do."

Red had been divorced for many years. He had two twin sons, seventeen years old, and two stepdaughters. The marriage had been difficult. His wife had some kind of bipolar problems and some kind of schizophrenia stuff going on. He said that when he first married her, she wasn't like that. He told me, "Diane, I'll always love her, but it was just too tough with her illnesses," and I said, "I get that."

Red's five years younger than me. He's forty-eight, and I'm fifty-three, but that's no big deal. In fact, that's good because I figure he won't die before me. Men tend to die earlier than women, so you don't want them to be older than you to start. It's funny how you think of stuff like that after you lose a husband.

At first, it was difficult with Red because it was like stepping back out there into the world of romance after so many years. William and I were together a really long time. I had many years of just one person, and now here's this other person. I wasn't used to dating.

Everybody in my church, if they're not married, hasn't had sex in ten or fifteen years. When I hear them talk about that, I'm about to fall on the floor. They're all women, and I'm saying to myself, "Everybody's emotionally constipated because they're waiting for this perfect Jesus man." God, forgive me for saying that. I love God, but you just can't live your life that way.

At one point, I got really fond of this married man at the church, but I would never, ever cheat. I would never mess with a marriage at all, but I was very fond of this person. So I was thinking, *I need to get these thoughts out of my head and put new thoughts in there.* I said, "God, you have to help me because I'm not into masturbation. I don't want to do that, but I do have needs." I realized I was starting to let William go emotionally. I mean, I will always love him. He will always be a part of my heart, but he does not live in this world anymore. He's in the spirit world, and he's never coming back.

I have to admit that Red is a sexy guy. I can appreciate a good-looking man with a nice personality. It's like when you have positive energy running in your heart, things just go right through, and it doesn't get blocked. But when you have some kind of pain, it's like your heart just constricts. My heart was still doing that. I told Red, "I want to be really fair to you. I don't want to be with you but be thinking about William the whole time." But he reassured me that we could take it slow, so we kept talking.

As Red and I talked on the phone, we started talking about intimacy issues and all that. I was thinking, *You're making me feel things that I haven't felt in a long time.* I hadn't had sex in six years. William and I stopped doing it almost two years before he died because he was so sick. I told Red, "Below my waist, my body is going crazy. My body is amazed." I said, "But above my waist, my heart is still conflicted." I don't know what I want. Part of me is saying, *It's time to move on. It's okay to love again.* The other part of me is saying, *You can't just play with someone's emotions. You can't string somebody along simply because you feel certain feelings.*

My body started waking up. I wasn't listening to my body before. My body was saying, "Hey! Pay attention to me!" One lady got up at church one day and announced, "I haven't had sex in nine years." First of all, that's a topic that should be between you and God. Second, that frightened me. I was thinking, *Okay, in nine years, I'll be freaking sixty-something.* My potential numbers are really going to be going down by then. It's crazy to think that way, but it's reality. I mean, look what's out there. As a woman who's fifty-three, there are not many choices. It's the guys who live with their mommas and the crazy alcoholics. There's not too much out there unless it's someone else who's lost a loved one, like Red did.

I realized Red had also gone through a grieving process similar to mine. His ex-wife definitely messed up in their relationship. I know her mental illness was part of the problem. He really grieved that loss. He said, "Diane, I don't expect you to not love William. He was a part of you. He was like your right arm, your right leg."

51

Red was very intuitive and spiritual. His parents were deceased. He lost his mother to diabetes, and his father died ten years later. He was very close to both of them, especially his father. One day, he asked me where William was buried, and I told him, "Down on the King Street extension, near downtown Charleston." He said, "Is it by an overpass?" I said, "Yeah. There's a tattoo shop nearby," and he said, "Oh, my God, that's where my mother is. You're a kindred spirit to me." He really believes that our spirits are connected.

We talked about sex before marriage. I try to live holy, and I think I do. I try not to hurt people. But I hadn't had a man put his arms around me in four years and just hold me, cuddle with me, soothe me, whatever you want to call it.

Anyway, Red told me, "Whatever you want to do is fine with me." So we went out a few times, and I was very attracted to his compassion for me. I asked him, "Why do you want me to call you Red? I know you told me that before, but now I'm wondering why." He said, "Because that's going to be our code word." I said, "What do you mean?" He said, "Whenever you say 'Red' to me, whatever I'm doing, I'm going to stop. If I'm saying the wrong thing, just say the word. If I'm touching you, and you don't want me to, all you have to do is say 'Red.'" I was thinking, *Well, no man has ever said that to me before. This is all very interesting!*

Since Red and I work in the same place, we had to really be

careful. I also told him, "I can't bring you to my house." Even though my children are not a product of divorce, they still lost their father. I know William had been dead for years, but I still worried that it could be confusing to have somebody else come into their lives. And I didn't know whether my relationship with Red would have real longevity. I didn't think it was right to introduce the kids to him until I was sure that we could go all the way to marriage one day.

So he said, "Well, what are we going to do?" And I said, "Well, I guess I'm going to have to come visit you." All this time, my mom is still living at my house, and she's driving me crazy sometimes. I'm thinking, *God, are you trying to tell me something? Maybe there's some benefit to her living with me?* So I decided to ask my mom to babysit my kids one night so I could go out with Red. I sat down, and I actually talked to her. Yes, I did. I reminded her that I was very angry with her about what had happened at church, but I had forgiven her. I finally decided that I was going to make myself be happy no matter what. No matter what struggle, no matter what challenge, no matter what trial and tribulation comes, I'm still going to find the happiness in something.

Even if, God forbid, a child of mine died, I'm still going to find happiness. It's all around me. There's trees, and there's air. I'm at that point because life is not promised to anybody. This is all a journey to eternity anyway. So I sat down with my mom and told her about Red. Well, guess who became my new cheerleader? She said, "Diane, you are only fifty-three. I am seventy-seven years old. When I got a hysterectomy, all the urges disappeared, so it doesn't bother me the way it's bothering you."

So I went to Red's house one night. I'm not sure what I was expecting. I had determined that I was going to make love to him because I wanted to, but I thought that I might end up crying. I wasn't sure what emotions to expect. I'm a big girl. I understand what the Bible says, and I prayed about it. I said, "God, you brought this man into my life." I did not go looking for him. I didn't. He is a very gentle soul, I mean, just an all-around nice guy. He loves kids, works at the school. I already knew that he didn't have a criminal record because he worked at the school.

Anyway, that night, we were talking and cuddling, and, well, one thing led to another. I'll just say it like that. We went all there. I was thinking, *Oh, my God!* as things progressed. My body was just out of control. I was really feeling it down there, and he noticed. I was thinking that I'm at the age where that kind of response was not supposed to happen, but it did. Big time. So it just kind of confirmed to me that this experience with Red was right. I realized that it's not normal to not have intercourse for such a long time.

So we did it that night, and I left to go back home. I didn't hear from him later that night. He did say, "I'll see you at work tomorrow." So the next day before I go to work, I'm looking on my phone, and there's no text. There's no "Hi," or "How are you doing?" I don't go to work until the afternoon, but the whole morning goes by with no text from him. I had already said to myself, *Diane, before you go over to his house, you have to make sure that this is absolutely one-hundred-percent what you want to do. This fellow could be giving you a line. You have to do it and have no regrets.*

So, I get to work at 1:45 p.m., and I run across him about an hour later. He has an office, and he kind of pulls me in there. He pops a kiss on my cheek and says, "How you doing?" I said, "Oh, don't say anything to me. You didn't even send me a text, even a 'hello' text." He said, "Girl, I've been watching you for the last forty-five minutes over in your office." I said, "What do you mean?" He said, "Don't tell anybody, but there's a school surveillance camera over where you are."

He said he was sitting at his desk, looking at me on the monitor, thinking about all the stuff we did last night. He said that after I went home, he looked at the sheets on his bed, and he just envisioned what we had been doing. He took a shower and went to sleep. He said he slept real good. I felt better when I heard all that.

I said, "We sound like little kids the way we're talking." Well, not really, since kids shouldn't have sex, but it was just really nice because we were two people who had gone through a lot in different ways. We actually made each other feel good. I felt like we'll always be friends even if the relationship goes nowhere else.

52

I really felt like I'd been blessed, and, yes, the church did help me. But—and this is a big but—if I go to Hell because I had sex with Red, then I guess I'm going to Hell because I'm not going to stop doing it. I'm not going to stop. I'm sorry, but I just felt so relieved. It's like the stress just disappeared. I didn't think about William one time. He didn't come into my mind one time. That's when I realized I had really released him and just come to terms with his death.

I believe that William would want me to be happy. I believe he'd say, "Okay, Diane, four years, that's a long time to grieve." I didn't see this coming. In fact, I was trying to protect myself and my heart. I had emotional walls up. I had been thinking that if I didn't give my heart to somebody, then I couldn't get hurt again.

For a while after William's death, I even acted that way with my kids too. I was shutting them out emotionally. I stopped calling my kids as much for a while. I used my classes and school as an excuse. I didn't realize what I was doing. Subconsciously, I was thinking that if I got close to my grandkids and something happened to them, I wouldn't be able to deal with it. So I didn't want to get close.

So now, every time I have sex, do I have to repent and say, "God, I'm sorry"? No. What I say is, "God, you know me. You know my heart. You wrote the book. You know what I'm going to do before I do it." I'm not trying to hurt anybody. I'm not messing with a married man. I'm not. We are two people who needed each other.

Red doesn't make a ton of money, but it's never been about money for me. A lot of women in the church—they're CNAs, certified nurse assistants. They got these minimum-wage jobs. I'm not trying to be mean, but I think they should be growing and building themselves so they can make the money they want to make. Instead, they're waiting for this wonderful rich person to come along. I feel sorry for them because they're going to go twenty years with no marriage and no sex because their priorities are wrong.

I live in the Bible Belt, so my apostle would kill me if he heard me talking about all this sex stuff. He would look at me and want to snatch me by my hair. I'm not sure how he's going to react when he reads all this stuff in the book. But not having sex is easier said than done. When I was grieving, it didn't bother me because I didn't care about sex. I didn't care about me. I just was so hurt, so depressed. I didn't even want to even dip my toe back in the water. I felt like if I don't fall in love, then I cannot be hurt again. But that attitude was a suffocation of my emotions and my sexuality, my everything. I didn't realize what I was doing.

I wasn't sleeping well before I met Red, but now I'm sleeping fine. I'm not kidding. I'm at peace. There's nothing whirling around in my head to keep me awake at night. I don't think about William nearly as much. I'm not thinking, *Oh William, I did this with Red, and you're going to be so mad at me.* One night, my mother said, "William is probably standing right there smiling at you now, Diane." Well, I know she meant well, but I don't think that's happening. William was very jealous. I let her say that, but I know that William's moved on. He's not here. He's void of consciousness. I haven't had any nightmares since I had sex with Red. I have just had fun.

Red curses, not every word, but he curses some. I actually told him, "Listen, I'm not trying to change you, but if you could just not curse in front of me, I would really appreciate that. I admit that four years ago, before I started going to church, I cursed like a sailor, but now I'm asking if you can just try not to do that." Red got defensive, saying, "I don't like anybody trying to change me," and all this and that. But after our talk, I noticed that he was actually trying not to curse, and I thought that was really cute. He made the effort, and that shows me that he cares how I feel about things.

One night, Red went to his son's football game. I should have told him I wanted to go with him, but I didn't. He didn't think I wanted to go, so he didn't ask me. Since I was on my own for the night, I went to Barnes and Noble to read. But after a while, I didn't want to stay there any longer. I thought, *Red's not going to be back at his house until about ten-thirty. So what am I going to do until then? Do I go home?* Then I remembered that the Coastal Carolina Fair was going on. I said to myself, "I need to go up to the fair and see what's going on up there."

That turned out to be very therapeutic for me. I hadn't been to the fair since William died. We used to go every year. The last two times we went, I had to put him in a wheelchair. We used to sit and watch the concerts, and I'd wrap him up in blankets. We'd drink hot chocolate.

It was eight dollars to get into the fair, so I paid and went in. I walked around, smelled wonderful stuff, and didn't eat anything. Really, I was just going to clear my mind. When I was there that night, I thought I would run into people I knew, but I didn't. I know that was God's doing. I realized this was meant to be my alone time for reflection. I enjoyed watching the arts and crafts shows, looking at the quilts that win the contests, and watching the crazy rides. I was in a safe place. I took a couple of pictures just to prove to my kids that I was actually at the fair on my own.

I certainly thought about William that night, but it wasn't horrible. It wasn't a hurting feeling. It felt like it was okay. Before I met Red, I don't think I could have gone to the fair with all those memories. I couldn't have done that. When William died, I laid prostrate on his grave and cried like a baby for weeks. Now, I can go to his grave and talk to him and not really cry at all. It's not that my heart doesn't cry. Of course, it does, but I realize that he's in a better place. He's in a spiritual place.

Later that night, after the fair, I went to Red's house, and we cuddled. He cooked for me, we sat and talked, and we went to sleep. We didn't even have sex. It's not a huge priority.

I know my pastors are not going to be happy when this is all written down, but I'm keeping it as real as I can keep it. I will tell anybody who listens, "Do not turn your back on God." I asked God to give me a husband. "I want a man who can be my husband. That's all I'm asking you for." And what does the Bible say? "If you don't ask, you don't get." I'm thinking, *God, you sent me my seventy-six-year-old mother. That's not what I asked for.*

My girlfriend, a minister, gave me a new way of looking at it. She said, "Diane, you accepted your mother. You forgave your mother, and God has rewarded you. Now you have a full-time babysitter."

53

Red was very kind, and he was very gentle, and he kind of just let me do my thing. As time went on, the sex continued to be great. I can't lie. He was one of the most caring people I know sexually. But he started to become afraid because I got very attached to him really fast. And he was probably right. I was extremely lonely in terms of companionship.

One night, he said to me, "Diane, I'm kind of scared that you're getting too involved with me emotionally, and I'm not there yet. It feels like I'm on chapter one, and you're on chapter nine. I don't want to hurt you." He was newly divorced, and it was not an easy marriage. Now he's on his own, and he said, "There are some things I really like about being single."

During his marriage, Red had woken up with this mean woman beside him for all those years. Now he's waking up alone, and he likes just being free. But I've been free for four-plus years now, and I don't want to be free anymore. I want to be attached to something, somebody. I really felt a strong attraction to Red.

One day, he said something about how he didn't want his neighbors to start thinking of me as his girlfriend because they were seeing me around his place so much. That stung. I said, "Wait a minute. I don't know if I told you this, but when I love, I love hard. I'm committed." I said, "I'll tell you how committed I am. When I found out William was HIV-positive, I stuck with him."

Red jumps up, "Wait a minute! Wait a minute! Wait a minute! William was HIV-positive?" I said, "Yeah, but I'm negative, so what's the problem?" He said, "No, you are not HIV-negative." I said, "Yes, I am negative." He asked, "How could you be so sure? You've never slipped? You never had sex with him without a condom?" I said to Red, "Let me tell you something. When you know someone's HIV-positive, you don't play around with that." I said, "We have eight children. William was not about to put me in any type of danger in terms of my HIV status." Well, I could tell Red was not happy with this new news. He goes, "I'm feeling some kind of way about this."

To tell the truth, Red and I did have unprotected sex. How it happened, I don't know. But I have to admit that it was kind of freeing. I had only had protected sex for twenty-something years. Did I think Red was HIV-positive? No, obviously, I didn't think he was HIV-positive. I'm thinking, *Okay, he's been married twenty years. They got a divorce, and there was no infidelity during that time.* I just went with the moment, and I realize that's not a good thing to do. In hindsight, that was very irresponsible on both our parts. But for my part, I knew I was HIV-negative.

Well, Red was very upset after this conversation. He kept saying, "I'm really feeling some kind of way about this." I said, "I'm trying to tell you I'm not HIV-positive. I would never have ever done that to you." But he's still feeling some kind of way. So the very next day, I went to the AIDS clinic on Dorchester Road because now I'm feeling upset. When I walked into that clinic, a flood of emotions hit me because this was the clinic where I had taken all of William's clothes after he died. They helped me pay my light bill after he died. They gave me some counseling after he died. And now I was back here at the same clinic to take an AIDS test myself.

I don't care how many times you take that test; there's still fear involved when you take it. You're thinking, *The results could be life-changing.* They were asking me, "Well, do you have somebody that can be here with you while you wait for the results of the test, just in case?" And I'm thinking, *My pastor, one of my pastors.* But then I said to myself, *I can't ask my pastors. They're going to freaking kill me because I'm not supposed to be having sex until I get married.* But they were the only two people I would even consider calling in a situation like that.

Then I decided, "I'm okay. Just go ahead. I don't need someone with me." Well, they do this little prick on the finger, a little five-minute thing, and they can tell you right then and there. They had me sign some papers, and I explained to them why I was doing the test. I was sitting with a very wonderful young counselor. He was maybe thirty years old. He was gay, and he told me that he had a partner who was HIV-positive, so he himself gets tested every six months. He said one time he had the flu, and he was scared to death because he thought it might be AIDS. But he was fine.

Before he did my test, I said, "My pastors are going to kill me because I've been having sex outside of marriage," and he said, "Diane, God is not a vengeful God. God is not going to punish you because you had sex." I thought about what he said. I said, "I did combat those urges for a long time, and I tried my very best." I did not want to sit there masturbating. That was just not my way. I had said, "God, you need to bring me a husband because, yes, I want to be a Christian, but I also want to have sex."

The counselor kept talking to me, and he was just being very, very sweet. Then, all of a sudden, he said, "You're negative."

It was like he let out all the air of the balloon I was carrying in my chest. I can't tell you how overwhelming it was. I just busted out crying. I was saying over and over, "Oh, my God. Thank you." Because, yes, I was scared. Really scared. I was scared because I hadn't taken that AIDS test in many years, and then I put myself at risk by having unprotected sex with Red.

Red and I did not have sex after that point. We talked, but he knew I still had strong feelings and emotions for him. One day, he said, "Give me a hug. Show me some love," so I gave him a hug. The next thing I know, he was hugging me in a way where he could have taken my clothes off if we were somewhere private. He didn't stick his hand in my shirt or anything, but I knew the physical attraction was still there. Maybe he was still struggling with that part of it. But I decided I didn't want things to go any further.

After I got tested, Red made a comment about AIDS that upset me. He said, "Since you're negative, I guess I'm negative." I told him, "Wow, I don't like that. You don't know for sure unless you get tested like I did." I said, "I'm a woman who knows her status, but you could be with other women who don't know their status, and they could be anything. You don't know what you're doing unless you take responsibility." I gave him that to ponder, and that's where we left it as far as the relationship goes.

Then I had an epiphany. Here it is. "Whoever loves the least in a relationship has the most power." I really do believe that.

EPILOGUE

My mom continued to live with me until she died.

At one point, I started having some vaginal bleeding. I went to the gynecologist because I hadn't had a period in years, and he did a biopsy. They put this real big, long needle into me. Thank God I was knocked out and didn't have to see anything. I hear it's painful, and that's why I was asleep. It turned out that I had endometrial cancer, and I needed surgery right away. I needed an emergency hysterectomy. I ended up with just one ovary left in my body. It was a serious operation. They said that I could have died if they had kept me on the operating table any longer.

I was having all sorts of radiation treatments afterward, so I couldn't go back to work. Well, I'll tell you what my mom did. She paid my entire mortgage until I could go back to work. I want to give my mother credit for that. She paid every bill I had while I was recuperating because I couldn't go to my job. She said, "Diane, I don't care. Just pay it." She was my strength as I was trying to recover from the cancer. She kept reassuring me, "You're going to be all right. You're going to be all right." I just felt so sick sometimes, but you can't cry in front of your kids. I didn't want to scare them. I didn't want them to think I wasn't going to make it. I would sit there in her room with her, and I would close the door. She had gotten a cat for company, and she would be petting her cat. I would just sit there with my head down, and she would say, "Don't cry. You're going to be all right. I'm here for you, and I'll make sure you're all right."

That behavior really started to change how I felt about her because she took care of me and my kids. My girls were also stepping up. They had a little money, and they were also doing things, buying food, stuff like that, because we didn't want to take advantage of my mom's generosity. But my mother told me, "Take whatever you need, anything you need." I had a special, expensive diet because I couldn't keep food down.

As things started changing between me and my mom, I started calling her "Ladybug." I don't know when or how that started, but I'd go in the room, and I'd be saying, "Hey, Ladybug, how are you doing?" She would tell me, "This is on TV, and that's on TV. I love looking out the window because you have so many trees." I had put a bird feeder out there so she could see the birds. I have woods all around me. She would lie there and say, "Diane, my cat is looking out the window. My cat has got a boyfriend out there." Looking at her, I said, "Mom, remember, your cat's name is David. If he has a boyfriend, I guess you've got two gay cats."

I remember one Halloween, she wanted to go and see all the kids who were out trick-or-treating, so I drove her around in different subdivisions and let her see the kids. She was just loving it. One of the people giving out candy said, "Can I help you?" I told him, "This is my mom. She's just enjoying watching the kids." He said, "Let me bring her a bag of candy." My mother was just in heaven. He brought her the candy and said, "That's so sweet that your mom wants to come out for Halloween," and she just loved it.

My mom's health started to decline as my health started to improve. When she became more bedridden, I didn't know what to do. I had never taken care of an elderly person. She started urinating on herself. I said, "Mom, why don't you just get up and go to the bathroom? It's right there." She had one of them chairs that lift you up. Matter of fact, she had two of them. She said, "Diane, I just can't hold it," so I got her Depends and all that kind of adult underwear.

What totally blew my mind was about six months later: she started defecating on herself. She had a little bit of dementia, but she was lucid most of the time. I said, "Mom why are you defecating on yourself? Don't you know you defecated? Don't you know you're sitting in it?" Inside me, I was thinking, *Oh, she's just doing this to drive me crazy.* But then it finally came to me: *Hello, knock on head. Of course, she doesn't know.* If she knew, she wouldn't be doing it.

One of my pastors was a nurse. She came over and showed me how to turn my mother correctly in the bed so she wouldn't get sores. She also showed me how to pull her up in the bed if I was there by myself. She gave me a wooden wedge that I put under her to transfer her and stuff like that. I mean, it was exhausting. I would say the last two years of my mom's life, I was just exhausted a lot of the time. I was absolutely tired.

One time, my mother tried to take a swing at me. It happened just out of the blue. She didn't like what I was telling her, and she tried to swat me. It was almost laughable. Can you imagine this seventy-nine-year-old trying to slap me? I got her by the arm, and I just held both of her arms. I didn't hold them tight, but I held them. And I said, "Let me tell you something. This will not happen. You will never touch me again in that way. If you touch me that way, I might lose my mind, and I don't want to do that. You know what I'm saying? Everything might come flooding back. All the memories." After about three hours, she apologized to me, and everything was okay then.

During the last two years, we got really, really close. And I really forgave her. I was changing her sheets one time, and her shit was all over me. I remember her saying, "You know, I should have been nicer to you when you were younger." She said this to me after the cancer scare and everything. I said, "Well, you're nice to me now. That's all that matters." I told her I forgave her, and when I said, "I forgive you," I meant it. I also said, "We're not going to talk about the past anymore."

There was a time when I hated her. I really did. I hated what she did to me. But that person I used to hate, I didn't see her anymore when I looked at my mom. I don't want other people to think of her that way. Yes, she was this horrible, horrible person at one time. But she was no longer that person, and our relationship did a complete 180 in those five years when she lived with me. I'm as amazed as anyone that such a change is possible, but I know it's God's will.

My mom had not been in great health, but her death came on suddenly. She was not feeling well, and we thought she had another urinary tract infection. I had a doctor come to our house, and they took a urine sample, and they told me she didn't have a urinary tract infection. So now I'm thinking, *Well, what's the matter with her?*

Then, a physical therapist who worked with her came by, and he listened to her heart. He said, "Hold on. I need to call my supervisor." He went outside and called them. Then, his supervisor came over and listened to her heart. She told me, "Your mother is passing." The word she actually used was "transitioning." I was like, "What?" I was shocked. After they left, I said to her, "Are you going to die on me?" I literally said that to her. She kept saying, "Let me sleep. Let me sleep." I said, "Mom, are you going to die on me?"

My mom passed away on January 2, 2019. The irony of the whole thing is that William passed away on January 4, 2009, almost exactly ten years earlier. They had to wheel his body from my bedroom, and then ten years later, they had to wheel my mother's body from her room on the other side of the house. We did hospice at home with both of them. How many families have to go through all that death in one house?

The one bright side of both deaths was that we got to spend another Christmas with both of them right before they died. For my mother, I made Christmas in her room because she was bedridden. I sent for Mary even though my mother hadn't spoken to her for five years. I said, "Mom, you have to forgive Mary for how she treated you." She said, "I'm not going to forgive her." I said, "You have to. If you want to go to heaven, you have to forgive her." I said, "You're dying, and you don't want to go to hell. You have to forgive her."

Finally, she said, "All right." And those were her words, "All right."

I called Mary. When we got on the phone, she started crying because she and I hadn't spoken in years. I was really angry with her for a long time. But I knew that my mother needed to forgive Mary because I wanted my mother to go to heaven. I really believe that there is an afterlife, the spiritual afterlife. I believe that wholeheartedly. I told my sister, "Don't you dare come here and say anything negative to her. If you say anything negative to her, then you've got to go immediately." Mary promised me she wouldn't do that, so I sent her the money for a plane ticket. When Mary came to my house, my mother literally opened her eyes, saw my sister, and smiled. She really did. I'm not kidding. I actually have a picture of that moment.

When my mother succumbed to being unconscious, I called my pastor. My mom loved my pastor. He used to call my mother "the queen." He would say, "How's my queen?" My mother was raised Catholic, so she called my pastor "Father," and nobody would get why she would call him "Father." But that's how they do it in the Catholic church. When my pastor's wife heard her say that, she said, "If you're going to call him 'Father,' then you have to call me 'Mother.'" And my mom said, "Well, okay, I'll call you 'Mother.'"

They loved her. They loved my mother. They came over to say goodbye and pay their last respects before she passed. At the time, she had been unconscious for at least thirty-six hours. My pastor went in there, and he held her hand and said, "How's my queen?" And she woke up. She said to him, "Father, what do you think God thinks of me now?" He patted her hand, touched her hair, and told her, "You did good. You did good."

She didn't come back to consciousness after that.

My oldest daughter Danielle knew that my mother was Catholic, and she went online and found a Catholic priest who could come to the house. He came to the house, and he did last rites for my mother while she was still unconscious. He also sang to her. He told her, "Miss Sharon, when you go to heaven, tell my parents hello." And he asked me what my mom's favorite song was, and I told him it was "Ave Maria." And he just started singing it. I'm telling you, this man could sing. I was floored, and then he left. It was like, one minute, he was here, the next minute, he was gone. But when he left the house, there was such a spiritual calmness in that room. We also played all these old records for my mother, like Tom Jones, all these things that my mother used to listen to, and just talked to her.

My mother wanted to be cremated, so I made the arrangements before she died. I was over at the funeral home finalizing things when Neil called me. He said, "Mom, you've got to get home right away." I was two minutes away from the house, and we had just finished signing the paperwork. But by the time I got home, my sister was out screaming in the street. I went inside, and my mom was gone. I was in shock because it seemed to happen so fast.

Given how our relationship started, it's hard to believe how it turned out. But she really did become my best friend. I miss her more as the years go by. I'm never going to see her again unless it's in heaven. That hits me once in a while.

We took her ashes on that ferry boat that goes out to Fort Sumter. It was cold, early January. My family went with me, and we spread my mom's ashes into the water. We let them go. But I kept some for myself in a little Ziploc bag beside my bed. I just have this feeling with her being in the drawer that she's still close to me. It's stupid because I know she's a spirit now. But I can't seem to let go of that tiny little bit of her that's in the Ziploc bag.

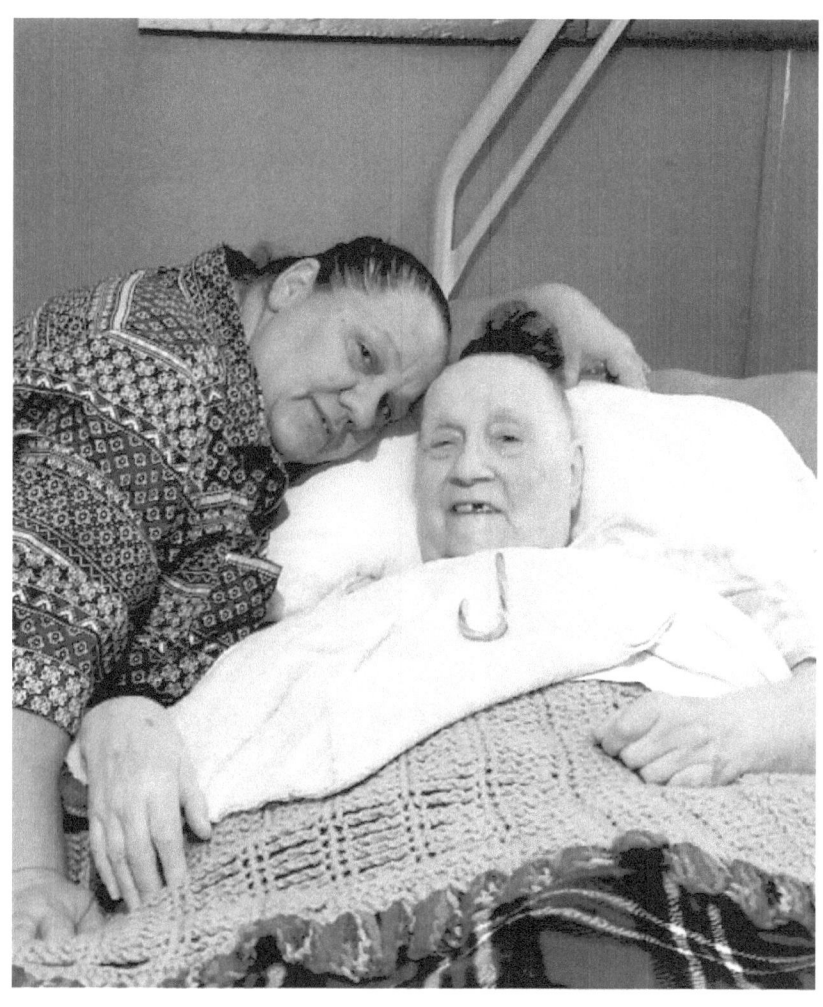

Diane with Sharon shortly before her death

AFTERWORD

EVEN THOUGH DIANE and I hadn't found anyone interested in publishing the book, she never lost faith that someday people would be able to read her story. We kept talking over the years, and I recorded my last interview with her in October 2020. The book remained a work in progress for both of us. I had a list of questions to ask her in our next meeting, hoping to fill in some of the gaps in her narrative.

We had trouble finding a time to meet, in part because Diane was struggling with health issues, including ascites (a condition where excess fluid collects in the abdomen). We spoke on the phone occasionally, but we didn't meet in person again.

I got this text from Diane in late February 2022: "Hi, Ward. I'm at Roper Hospital downtown. I've had another ascites attack, and the doctors are doing two more biopsies. I'm feeling pretty bad. Keep me in your prayers."

I told her I wanted to visit her, but she got transferred to a different hospital. She became less responsive to my texts, but I figured we would catch up once she fully recovered and regained her strength.

A couple of weeks later, her daughter Danielle called and told me that Diane had died. The doctors discovered belatedly that she was suffering from late-stage liver cancer rather than just ascites. This news came as a shock to everyone in her life.

Attending Diane's funeral was a meaningful but somewhat surreal event. In all the years we'd known each other, we had never met each other's families. I certainly felt like I had gotten to know her family through our conversations, but nothing prepared me for seeing them in person. Suddenly, I'm in the same room as her children, her sister, and even Will (the father of two of her children). I could feel Diane's presence all around us. It was a very powerful experience.

Seeing all these people from Diane's life for the first time made her story seem even more real, but now I had a big decision to make. Should I proceed with the book or just let it go? After much thought and prayer, I came to believe that Diane would want to move forward and share her story. I felt like she had bequeathed me these words. Although I could no longer consult with her about the next steps, I felt like she was guiding me along the way.

I chose to wait a year after her death before reaching out to her family to get their thoughts. They knew she had been working with me on a book, but they had never seen any drafts. I sent them the latest version to review. Obviously, I knew that some of Diane's intimate and unfiltered recollections might be difficult for them to read. Despite that, they generously gave me the approval to proceed with the book, and I am very grateful for their support. Now that I had her family's consent, it renewed my determination to find a way to publish her story, and that's how you're reading it now.

Even though Diane will never see this, I want to express my profound appreciation to her for trusting me with her life story. I'm so glad we happened to sit next to each other in class that day thirteen years ago. If you found some strength or inspiration from reading this book, I know Diane would be happy.

Ward V.B. Lassoe

www.ingramcontent.com/pod-product-compliance
Lightning Source LLC
LaVergne TN
LVHW041930070526
838199LV00051BA/2765